The Dismissal Dossier

Everything You Were Never Meant To Know About November 1975

Jenny Hocking

16

EasyRead Large

(RHYW)

Copyright Page from the Original Book

MELBOURNE UNIVERSITY PRESS
An imprint of Melbourne University Publishing Limited
Level 1, 715 Swanston, Carlton, Victoria 3053, Australia
mup-contact@unimelb.edu.au
www.mup.com.au

First published 2015
Updated edition published 2016; reprinted 2016
This updated edition published 2017
Text © Jenny Hocking, 2017
Design and typography © Melbourne University Publishing Limited, 2017

Cover design by Philip Campbell Design
Text design and typesetting by Cannon Typesetting
Printed in Australia by McPherson's Printing Group

National Library of Australia Cataloguing-in-Publication entry

Hocking, Jenny, author.

The dismissal dossier: everything you were never meant to know about November 1975/Jenny Hocking.

9780522873009 (paperback)
9780522873016 (ebook)

Whitlam, Gough, 1916–2014.
Australian Labor Party—History—20th century.
Australia—Politics and government—1972–1975.

324.29407

TABLE OF CONTENTS

Praise for *The Dismissal Dossier*

'*The Dismissal Dossier* is shocking, compelling, and profoundly important. It is a constitutional horror story, in which democratic process is the victim, and the perpetrators got away with it. Jenny Hocking's impressive research and analysis should dispel a forty-year fiction perpetrated on the Australian public: that the Prime Minister didn't have a political solution, and that Sir John Kerr acted alone. Instead, Kerr acted with the foreknowledge and implied consent of the Queen, and in concert with the Chief Justice of the High Court of Australia, another High Court Judge and the Leader of the Opposition to oust a democratically elected government. That these actors in the drama were able to conceal the true history is shocking. Hocking's book is an important reminder about the vulnerability of democratic process, a revelatory account of the events of 1975 and, hopefully, a wise contribution for when we draft the constitution of the Republic of Australia.'

Anna Funder

ii

'*The Dismissal Dossier* is short, but its content is nothing less than mind-blowing. It is a must-read, not only for lefties maintaining the rage, but for everyone with a stake in the Australian democratic process.'
Joseph Sampson, *Law Society Journal*

Praise for *Gough Whitlam: A Moment in History*

'It lets us see who Gough Whitlam the person was before he became Gough Whitlam the politician ... We learn a lot along the way through the pages of this biography. And could I say it is an elegantly written and elegantly crafted biography.'
The Hon. Kevin Rudd, Launch of *Gough Whitlam: A Moment in History,* 6 November 2008

'This is the first instalment in what shapes up to be the best Australian political biography in decades. Monash University research professor Jenny Hocking has crafted a wonderfully detailed, but never boring, story of the man many consider to be the most charismatic prime minister this nation has ever had.'
Greg Kelton, *Adelaide Advertiser*

'It is a testament to Hocking's research, her eye for the apt example, and her scholarship that she is able to expand our understanding of the man,

and the influences that shaped such a significant Australian figure.'
Carmen Lawrence, *Overland,* no.194, Autumn 2009

Praise for *Gough Whitlam: His Time*

'A monumental project of several years' duration reminiscent of the glory days of publishing.'
Judges, Barbara Ramsden Award, 2014 Fellowship of Australian Writers National Literary Awards

'Professor Jenny Hocking's remarkable second volume of her Gough Whitlam biography [has] enough fresh material and new angles to keep alive the intrigue with this period of our history, even for the aficionados.'
Richard Ackland, *Sydney Morning Herald,* 31 August 2012

'A fascinating and important account ... and a tour de force as a piece of history.'
Associate Professor Frank Bongiorno, ANU, *Canberra Times,* 9 October 2012

'Hocking creates a rounded portrait of a complex and flawed idealist ... her picture of Whitlam makes his government's wild ride seem entirely

appropriate to the times and even more exciting in retrospect.'
Short Takes, *Herald Sun,* 10 November 2012

'There is no better account of how the triumph of 1972 turned into the catastrophe of 1975.'
Neal Blewett, *Australian Book Review,* November 2012

'It's time ... to hand Jenny's book over to the Australian people for them to draw their own conclusions.'
Hon. Gough Whitlam

PROFESSOR JENNY HOCKING FASSA is Australian Research Council, Discovery Outstanding Researcher Award (DORA) Professorial Fellow with the National Centre for Australian Studies at Monash University and the inaugural Distinguished Whitlam Fellow at the Whitlam Institute at the University of Western Sydney. She is the author of the acclaimed two-volume biography of Gough Whitlam, an award-winning biographer and scriptwriter and a regular media commentator on Australian politics and political biography.

Gough Whitlam: His Time was awarded the Fellowship of Australian Writers' Barbara Ramsden Award in 2014. It was shortlisted for the Prime Minister's Literary Awards (National History Prize) 2013, the Queensland Literary Awards 2013, longlisted in the Nib Waverley Awards for Literature 2013 and a finalist in the 2013 National Biography Award. *Gough Whitlam: A Moment in History* was shortlisted for the *Age* Book of the Year 2009, the Queensland Premier's Literary Awards and the Prime Minister's Awards for

Literature 2009, longlisted for the Walkley Awards Non-Fiction Book Award 2009 and a finalist in the 2010 Magarey Medal for Biography.

Jenny Hocking is also the author of the major biographies *Lionel Murphy: A Political Biography,* shortlisted in the Adelaide Festival Awards for Literature: National Non-Fiction Awards; and *Frank Hardy: Politics Literature Life,* shortlisted in the NSW Premier's History Awards. She has also written extensively on counterterrorism and democracy, including *Terror Laws: ASIO, Counter-terrorism and the Threat to Democracy.*

'*Occasionally words must serve to veil the facts. But let this happen in such a way that no-one become aware of it.*'

Niccolò Machiavelli

UNCOVERING A HIDDEN HISTORY

THE DISMISSAL OF the Whitlam government on 11 November 1975 by the Governor-General Sir John Kerr has always been as much about myth as reality. No single episode in our political history has been as thoroughly traversed as this. Yet despite the wealth of material—the microscopic dissections of meetings, conversations, legal and political arguments before, during and after Kerr's actions—the history was never really settled. It had always seemed to me that the dismissal could never be understood so long as it was presented in isolation from the trajectory of the Whitlam government itself, seen as the outcome of a four-week political crisis that began when the Opposition first blocked Supply in the Senate on 16 October 1975, rather than as the culmination of three years of sustained destabilisation and obstruction that had begun with the election of the first Labor government in twenty-three years. The historical perspective was simply wrong and so too was the dismissal narrative it had created. It had distorted the history and worse, obscured some of its most critical elements.

Although I had long believed that the history of the dismissal was incomplete nothing could have prepared me for the shock of finding, after thirty-seven years, among the largely untouched private papers of Sir John Kerr in the National Archives of Australia, the astonishing revelation of his secret meetings with the then High Court Justice Sir Anthony Mason and of Mason's involvement in the dismissal. Remarkable as these revelations were for our understanding of the dismissal, they held equally compelling implications for our understanding of history. How is it possible that something as significant as this—lengthy secret interactions between the Governor-General and a High Court judge at such a critical time—could have remained secret for thirty-seven years? What does it tell us about our presumptions of the 'received history' of the dismissal, and about the fragility of history?

The revelation about the role of Sir Anthony Mason, first published in *Gough Whitlam: His Time* in 2012, was just one of several defining aspects of the dismissal of the Whitlam government that had been variously overlooked, concealed, or simply forgotten as the history took shape. A powerful mix of political imperative, historical amnesia and deliberate distortion had generated lasting confusion and ignorance about some of the most critical elements. Without them, our knowledge and understanding of the dismissal remains incomplete. Five key aspects, each one central to the dismissal yet too frequently absent from its history, are to be explored here: Kerr's extensive communications with the Palace; his private contact with the Leader of the Opposition Malcolm Fraser; his secret interactions with High Court Justice Sir Anthony Mason; Gough Whitlam's crucial decision to call a half-Senate election; and the post-dismissal Parliamentary sitting, on the afternoon of 11 November 1975, during which the House of Representatives passed a motion of no confidence in Malcolm Fraser and called on the Governor-General to re-commission the Whitlam government.

By recalling these key elements from historical obscurity and placing them at the heart of our understanding and analysis of the dismissal, this book brings a new and important perspective to it and lays bare the collusion and the deception at its core. *The Dismissal Dossier* reveals for the first time the remarkable claims made by former Prime Minister Malcolm Fraser and former Liberal Senator Reg Withers in previously embargoed interviews, together with original archival research and contemporaneous records, and further exploration of Sir John Kerr's private papers—many of which remain unopened. The dismissal continues to give up its secrets in a series of gradual and resisted revelations that have filled out, if not yet completed, the story of the dismissal of the Whitlam government. A new narrative can now be seen, emerging from the shadows of one of the most controversial actions in our political history.

Since this book was first published in 2015, the history of the dismissal has undergone further dramatic revision, with an increasing focus on the possible role of the Palace. For too long the obvious nexus—between the Queen and her representative in Australia—has been overlooked as a factor worthy of any serious consideration in the dismissal, despite Kerr's resuscitation of the prerogative powers of the Crown that enabled it. Lumped in with the 'usual suspects'—the CIA, MI6, ASIO—as mere conspiracy, the Palace connection has been routinely ignored. Kerr's immediate protestation, that in dismissing Whitlam he had 'protected' the Queen and had ensured the Palace was not involved, has been too readily accepted and too little questioned. Until now.

There is a critical element in the evolving dismissal history that remains to be told; the Palace connection. Speculation over the possible involvement of the Palace in Kerr's deliberations has intensified with the refusal of the National Archives of Australia, Government House, and Buckingham Palace, to release the

'Palace letters'. These letters, between Kerr and the Queen, her private secretary, Sir Martin Charteris, and Prince Charles in the months before the dismissal, are embargoed by the Queen until at least 2027, with her private secretary retaining a veto over their release even after that date. In other words, we may never see this correspondence unless the Palace says we can. This is an extraordinary situation, a denial of our sovereignty and a rejection of our right to know and have access to critical documents in our own history.

With access to these significant historical records denied to us, I initiated an action in the Federal Court of Australia against the National Archives of Australia in 2016, seeking the release of the Palace letters. This historic case has been driven by a crowd-funding campaign through Chuffe d.org, and with a significant legal team working on a *pro bono* basis—led by senior barrister Antony Whitlam, QC, with Tom Brennan, and instructed by Corrs Chambers Westgarth in Sydney. While the judge has reserved his decision, which is expected to be handed down as this revised edition goes to press, any possible release of the Palace letters could be some months away, regardless of the outcome. The case has already made history as the final decision over the release of the Palace letters will now be made by an Australian court according to Australian law, and not by the Queen.

The refusal to release the Palace letters short of legal challenge simply continues the secrecy and distortion that has marked the history of the dismissal for decades. The withholding of the Palace letters continues the pattern of quasi-colonial historical condescension detailed in this book, and it deserves to be challenged. At the same time the pursuit of the Palace letters has pointed to a broader Palace connection, to be found in the files of the Foreign and Commonwealth Office (FCO) in the UK National Archives. What these files reveal is profoundly disturbing and places the dismissal in an entirely new light, one in which the British authorities played a critical role. They show a pattern of secrecy, even deception, of the Australian government and its Prime Minister, Gough Whitlam, as he moved to call the 1975 half-Senate election and reveal the secret planning by the FCO to approach Kerr to intervene, in order to 'protect' the Queen.

PROEM

AS THE PRIME Minister, Gough Whitlam, pulled into the driveway of Yarralumla at 1pm on 11 November 1975 he was, for the first time in four tumultuous weeks, calm, confident and totally at ease. In his top pocket was his formal letter to the Governor-General, Sir John Kerr, advising the half-Senate election that he had finalised with Kerr over the previous five days and confirmed with him just that morning. The draft documents had been received by Government House and the date had been agreed—13 December 1975.[1] As Whitlam's car drew up at the Prime Minister's entrance to Yarralumla, ABC radio was running a special edition of its afternoon current-affairs program, *PM,* covering the dramatic development that the Prime Minister was to announce a half-Senate election as soon as parliament resumed after lunch.[2] Whitlam's short speech to the House of Representatives announcing the half-Senate election had already been written, ready for delivery later that day. The 'crisis' in the Senate was over.

An ebullient Whitlam had entered his party room meeting that morning to rousing cheers from a weary caucus, their exuberance confirming his belief in his superior political strategy, his refusal to bend to the absurd demands of the Senate and his party's perseverance. Three times the government had tried to bring their budget bills forward for a vote in the Senate and three times the Liberal/National Country Party Coalition had refused to allow their Senators to vote on them.[3] And there they had remained, stuck in political limbo with the Senate 'on strike', as Whitlam described it. The half-Senate election had always been Whitlam's ultimate strategic end-point, as he had articulated to an enthusiastic caucus at the beginning of the crisis. Should the budget bills remain blocked he would bring forward the half-Senate election, then due any time before 1 July 1976, and call the Opposition out on a political crisis entirely of its own making.[4]

The few opinion polls commissioned during the crisis pointed to the surety of Whitlam's strategy. From a high point in mid-October 1975, Leader of the Opposition Malcolm Fraser's political stocks had declined over each week of the crisis and were falling more quickly the longer the stand-off in the Senate continued. By the second week of November support for Fraser was at an all-time low, with a 10 per cent increase in support for the government since the Appropriation Bills had first been blocked and 64 per cent of people disagreeing with the Coalition's actions.[5] Just that morning *The Bulletin* had set its presses rolling with the front-page story, 'Malcolm: the Man in the Muddle', pondering how the political career of Malcolm Fraser had come to such an unedifying self-inflicted conclusion.

And so Whitlam entered the Governor-General's study that afternoon with his mind on the mechanics of the half-Senate election, on the Labor party's need to fund its third election campaign in as many years and on the imponderable question of the outcome. The party's national secretary was already booking the campaign launch in the Sydney Opera House as Whitlam sat down to face Kerr. Reaching into his pocket he took out the letter they had discussed the previous week and confirmed again that morning, 'I have the letter advising the half-Senate election', he said, handing his written advice to the Governor-General. He was momentarily confused, stunned, as Kerr interrupted him and turned away from his outstretched hand. He watched as if in slow motion as the Governor-General bent down heavily and picked up a letter from his desk, where it was waiting face down and already signed. 'Before you say anything', Kerr said, turning back to him, 'I want to say something to you ... I have decided to withdraw your commission'. Whitlam listened and read the letter in disbelief: 'I hereby determine your appointment as my chief adviser and head of the government ... I propose to send for the Leader of the Opposition and to commission him to form a new caretaker Government'.[6] Whitlam later described it as the greatest shock he had ever experienced. 'We will all have to live with this', Kerr said. 'You certainly will', Whitlam replied, before shaking Kerr's hand and leaving.

***

ON THE MORNING of 11 November 1975 the Governor-General, Sir John Kerr, had placed a telephone call to the Leader of the Opposition, Malcolm Fraser. In itself this telephone call was scandalous, even treacherous. It was made in secret, without the knowledge of the Prime Minister, Gough Whitlam, and in contravention of the Constitutional requirement that the Governor-General act on the advice of his ministers.[7] Its contents were even more incendiary. Together, the Governor-General and the Leader of the Opposition conferred on the removal of Whitlam as Prime Minister later that day and the appointment of Fraser as Prime Minister in his place despite the facts that his party had lost the previous two elections, that Fraser himself did not have the confidence of the House of Representatives, and could never secure it. Four of Fraser's closest colleagues were with him when the call came through and watched in astonishment as he jotted down four points—the terms on which Kerr would hand government to the Opposition and appoint Fraser Prime Minister.

If the Governor-General was to have such a conversation about the formation of government, it should surely have been with the Prime Minister, Gough Whitlam, his chief adviser and the leader of the party elected to government. To do otherwise was to deny this most fundamental relationship in the democratic process and usurp the role of the electorate in the formation of government. Aware of the enormity of this conversation, the significance of the Governor-General and the Leader of the Opposition conferring without the knowledge of the Prime Minister—and on the removal of that Prime Minister—when faced with questions about it by quizzical journalists later that day, Fraser and Kerr simply lied: 'totally false', Kerr retorted.[8] When Fraser was asked whether he had any prior knowledge of the dismissal of the Whitlam government, he was insistent;

'No, none at all'. He appeared indignant at the mere suggestion.[9]

It was not until a decade later that Fraser and Kerr's shared story, their agreed historical confabulation, publicly unravelled. The once tight political partnership of Malcolm Fraser and his former Senate leader, Reg 'Toe-cutter' Withers, had fallen apart barely three years after the dismissal, when Fraser dismissed Withers himself from the ministry, leaving a spurned and bitter colleague with a great deal to tell. Their split came at a most inopportune time for Fraser, just as the former Labor minister Clyde Cameron was setting out to record a series of 'reminiscential' [sic] conversations with political figures for the National Library of Australia. Withers and Cameron were old political foes who had become friends, and Withers later confided the truth to Cameron about Fraser and Kerr's clandestine phone call on the morning of 11 November 1975. Cameron took great delight in referring to Withers' remarks, forcing Fraser to finally acknowledge his conversation with Kerr, his agreement to the terms and his prior knowledge of the dismissal—all of which he had previously steadfastly denied for the previous decade. 'The truth', Fraser now rather querulously suggested, 'is very important ... in its proper form'.[10] Not so for Kerr, who continued to deny that this conversation with Fraser establishing the terms on which he would take office had taken place on the morning of 11 November 1975, or that he had come to any arrangement with the Leader of the Opposition, before the dismissal of Gough Whitlam.

This 'thumping lie' was just one of the many historical fictions—a mixture of errors, omissions and outright fabrications—which quickly defined the story of the dismissal of the Whitlam government. It would drive a false narrative for decades, an established history built on quicksand and masking a hidden history of the dismissal—the story we were never meant to know.

The popular view of what became known simply as 'the dismissal' went something like this:

Faced with plummeting electoral support, beset by ministerial sackings, cruelled by unconventional and possibly illegal financial dealings, and with the economy in a tailspin, the Whitlam Labor government was dealt a final blow when the Opposition Coalition Senators refused to pass its budget. As the Senate repeatedly blocked the Supply bills, Whitlam's 'crash through or crash' political approach drove his determination to 'break the Senate' in a game of political brinkmanship that saw him face off against the equally tall, austere and steely determination of the Leader of the Opposition, the Liberal party leader, Malcolm Fraser. As Whitlam clung to power, refusing to do the decent thing and call an election or resign, the Governor-General Sir John Kerr was forced to act in order to 'solve the crisis' and 'save Australia'. Malcolm Fraser now committed to passing Supply, which the Senate duly did, and announced a double dissolution election at which the voters delivered an overwhelming verdict in support of the Governor-General and Fraser's actions.

The critical elements in this popular representation of the dismissal took form at once, fuelled by ignorance, disbelief and uncertainty, and filtered through the interstices of deception. They can be seen in the Minutes of the British Cabinet meeting of 11 November 1975, where, within hours of Whitlam's dismissal, the Foreign and Commonwealth Secretary reported with masterful understatement on recent events in Australia:

> The Governor General, Sir John Kerr, had taken the unusual step of dismissing the Prime Minister, Mr Whitlam, because of his refusal to resign following rejection of his budget by the Senate ... In place of Mr Whitlam's Administration, the Governor General had appointed a caretaker Government, whose task it was to vote Supply and then call a General Election. The situation which had arisen in no way involved the United Kingdom Government. The Governor General was

responsible to The Queen in her capacity as Queen of Australia.[11]

With this potted story the flawed historical record had begun in earnest. It was wrong on almost every point: the budget had not been 'rejected' it had not yet been voted on; the Governor General's action was not 'unusual', it was unprecedented; and Whitlam had not 'refused to resign' since there had been no call for him to do so, and he had already informed Kerr that he was to advise a half-Senate election. Finally, the Cabinet brief did not indicate that the 'caretaker' Government referred to was not a Labor government led by a Prime Minister other than Whitlam, but a new administration made up of the Opposition parties and with the Leader of the Opposition now installed as Prime Minister, without the confidence of the House of Representatives.

This British Cabinet overview, erroneous though its key points were, nevertheless established what would become the lasting and insistent elements in the popular narrative of the dismissal. Its final coda pointed to one further critical element in this historical mirage: that Kerr's actions in no way involved the Queen. The Queen's private secretary, Sir Martin Charteris, fuelled this view in his letter to the Speaker of the House, Gordon Scholes, after the dismissal, stressing the sole jurisdiction of the Governor-General: 'Her Majesty, as Queen of Australia, is watching events in Canberra with close interest and attention, but it would not be proper for her to intervene in person in matters which are so clearly placed within the jurisdiction of the Governor-General by the Constitution Act'.[12] Kerr's detailed 'Statement of Reasons' released the day after the dismissal made no mention of the Queen as having any place in his considerations nor revealed any interactions by him with her or with the Palace.[13]

The view that the Palace had no advance knowledge of and no involvement in Kerr's deliberations continues to hold firm as one of the few apparently uncontested facts about the dismissal. It was a position steadfastly maintained by Kerr, as he wrote in his memoirs, 'The decisions I took were without the Queen's advance knowledge'. Decades later the view that the Queen had no advance knowledge of even the possibility of dismissal and no involvement persisted, with Sir William Heseltine, then assistant private secretary to the Queen, suggesting that the Palace was 'disappointed Kerr didn't consult the Queen about what he intended to do'.[14]

Even Gough Whitlam himself, reflecting on these events in an interview for BBC television in 2002, believed that Kerr had misled the Queen as well as him, that Kerr had at no stage contacted the Palace about his dismissal. If the Queen had known of even the possibility of his dismissal, Whitlam reasoned, it could never have happened. 'If Kerr had got in touch with the Queen before doing it, it wouldn't have happened. Her immediate reaction would have been, "Have you consulted your Prime Minister?" or "What is your Prime Minister's advice?". I mean, do you doubt that she would have said that?', he asked, rather hopefully.[15] Well, yes and no. That Whitlam's faith in political and institutional propriety remained unbroken, despite the evidence of his own experience, will always be one of the most remarkable human elements in this otherwise tawdry story.

1

WHAT DID THE PALACE KNOW?

IT WAS OF course a preposterous fiction. Kerr had kept the Palace informed since September of his thinking and, most significantly, that he was considering dismissing Whitlam. The only point on which the Palace was not informed, according to Kerr, was the date on which he acted against Whitlam—leaving it open for Kerr to later exercise the sophistry that the Palace had 'no advance knowledge' of the date on which he dismissed Whitlam: 'I did not tell the Queen in advance that I intended to exercise these powers *on 11 November.*'[1] In fact the Palace had clear advance knowledge that the dismissal of Gough Whitlam was precisely what Kerr was considering.

Yet in October, with the Supply bills blocked in the Senate, Kerr conveyed quite a different view to Whitlam. In response to mounting pressure on him to act unilaterally against the government, Kerr told the Prime Minister that he did not accept the arcane notion of discretionary vice-regal 'reserve powers'. A relieved Whitlam told his colleagues of Kerr's view of the existence of the reserve powers; 'He thinks it's bullshit'![2]

In a handwritten journal from 1980, which I located in 2010 among Kerr's private papers held by the National Archives of Australia, Kerr sets out his discussions with the Palace during this time. Kerr had spoken to Prince Charles personally on more than one occasion as early as August 1975, canvassing the dismissal of Whitlam; Kerr was writing regular and extended letters to the Queen and to Charteris and had been assured that the Queen received and read every one of them. 'I was told by both him [Charteris] and the Queen that it was all read by the Queen and she herself told me that if I found the need to write to her direct to feel entirely at liberty to do so.'[3]

It is through Kerr's own description of his conversations with Prince Charles and others at the Palace, located in his private papers in the National Archives, that we now know that the Palace was well aware that Kerr was considering dismissing Whitlam as the Opposition moved ineluctably toward blocking Supply in the Senate. Kerr recounts Prince Charles's solicitous response to the Governor-General's concern for his own possible recall by Whitlam, should Whitlam hear that Kerr was even contemplating this: 'But surely Sir John, the Queen should not have to accept advice that you should be recalled at the very time should this happen *when you were considering having to dismiss the government'.*[4]

Central to Kerr's communications with the Palace was this fear for his own position, that Whitlam might replace him as Governor-General if he knew of Kerr's intention to dismiss him—although there is no indication Whitlam ever actually attempted to do so, even when faced with dismissal on 11 November 1975. Throughout these exchanges the Palace and Kerr discuss events in the clear context of the Governor-General's consideration of the dismissal of the Whitlam government. So frank were these conversations that just one week before the dismissal, Charteris wrote to Kerr advising him on the matter closest to the Governor-General's heart—his own job security. Charteris informed Kerr of the Queen's intentions should Whitlam move to recall him as Governor-General before Kerr had had the opportunity to dismiss Whitlam. Kerr's later description of this in his journal makes its import clear: 'I knew what the Palace view was as to what the Queen's ultimate reaction to the problem would have to be'.

In an astonishing exchange, Kerr records that Charteris told him that should this 'contingency' occur, the Queen would 'try to delay things' for as long as possible, although, Charteris acknowledged, 'in the end the Queen would have to act on the advice of her Prime Minister'. It is clear from this critical discussion that first, the Palace had failed to inform Whitlam of the nature of these secret communications with the Governor-General and, in particular, that Kerr was considering the option of dismissal; second, Kerr had established in advance the response of the Palace to the prospective dismissal of the Whitlam government; and third, the Palace had informed Kerr that in the event of Whitlam advising Kerr's recall, the Queen would not immediately act and would instead delay things for as long as possible. On all three counts this was critical information for the Governor-General to know in advance of taking such unparalleled action. Most importantly for Kerr the Palace had, according to his account, raised no objection to the prospect of the dismissal of the Whitlam government.

It is impossible to overstate the significance of this exchange. Not only had the Palace been kept closely and secretly informed by Kerr that he was considering dismissing the Whitlam government, the Palace had also confirmed with Kerr their response should Whitlam first move to recall him as Governor-General. It establishes a secret arrangement between the Palace and the Governor-General to delay acting on the advice of the Australian Prime Minister to recall the Governor-General, a decision fully within the power and responsibility of the Prime Minister to make. Given that the context to this exchange was Kerr's consideration of dismissing Whitlam, by agreeing to delay the hypothetical recall of the Governor-General for as long as possible, the Palace had agreed to give Kerr the maximum time in which to act to finalise that dismissal. The implication of this vital exchange makes a mockery of Charteris's concluding reminder that, in the end, the Queen would have to act on the advice of her Prime Minister; the question is, by that stage, just who would the Prime Minister be?

This extraordinary vice-regal manoeuvring presents Whitlam as a political ingénue, utterly unaware that among those he considered nothing more than postcolonial monarchical relics, his future as the head of elected government was being determined with all the calculated anti-democratic sentiment of monarchs through the ages.

***

IN THE HEAT of early spring 1975 in the New Guinea highlands,

Governor-General Sir John Kerr sidled up to Prince Charles and suggested a quiet chat. Their topic? The possible dismissal of the Prime Minister, whose guest at the Papua New Guinea Independence Day celebrations they both were. Kerr's prime concern in confiding this exceptional matter of state to the Prince was, as ever, his own job security. His focus was not on national governance, matters of vice-regal propriety or political probity but his personal tenure, his repeated concern that if he discussed these matters with Whitlam then the Prime Minister would immediately contact the Palace and have him recalled. In the aftermath of the dismissal Kerr presented his fear as redemptive fact, and Whitlam as playing entirely to type.

This is something Kerr consistently claimed—in his memoirs he described Whitlam's immediate reaction to the dismissal as a wild-eyed and frantic race to contact the Palace—and itself a personal *post-hoc* validation for Kerr's actions: 'Things then happened as I had foreseen. Mr Whitlam jumped up, looked urgently around the room, looked at the telephones and said sharply, "I must get in touch with the Palace at once".'[5] Although Kerr maintained this view until the end, it remains unsupported by the evidence. Palace staff later confirmed that Whitlam did not contact the Palace until early in the evening of 11 November, Australian time, at which point he made no reference to the possibility of Kerr's recall, and told the Queen's staff, 'I am no longer Prime Minister'.[6]

The first contact made with the Palace came not from Whitlam, but from the Governor-General's own staff, one hour after the dismissal. In 2010 I interviewed Bill Denny, one of the three servicemen then being considered for the position of *aide-de-camp* at Government House, and who had unexpectedly found themselves in the middle of these historic events. They had been invited to lunch with Sir John and Lady Kerr on 11 November, after drinks in the small drawing room. The Governor-General drank gin and tonic, before leaving to dismiss Whitlam and install Fraser. Kerr then arrived at lunch late and flushed, and rapidly consumed a large amount of alcohol. Denny recalls that the official secretary, David Smith, interrupted these baroque proceedings to ask whether anybody had contacted the Palace. Far from this being at the forefront of Kerr's mind, as might have been expected had Whitlam already been frantically searching for a telephone to do just that, a now obviously drunk Kerr replied that the Palace had not been contacted. Lady Kerr, in an assumption of Vice-Regal authority, then directed Smith to do so. By this time it was, according to both Denny and Smith, shortly after 2pm.[7]

Kerr's claim that Whitlam immediately tried to contact the Palace now stands alone as a slightly absurd caricature. It matches neither the facts nor Whitlam's determined, near obsessional, concern for institutional rectitude. Whitlam later described it as a 'concoction'.[8] It is difficult to imagine anything that Whitlam would be *less* likely to do than desperately try to contact the Palace to seek Kerr's removal, and he did not. Kerr's imagined certainty that Whitlam would 'race to the Palace' to recall him in reality came to nothing; it reflected only Kerr's own insecurities and the need to vindicate his decision to deceive Whitlam and 'to remain silent to him'.[9]

Former High Court Justice Michael Kirby later delivered an excoriating assessment of Kerr's personal and political ethos in repeatedly citing concerns for his own position in dismissing Whitlam without warning:

> This wasn't, in my view, the honest, honourable, direct way the Crown acts ... The excuse given at the time was that had Sir John Kerr alerted Mr Whitlam to what he was thinking of doing, Mr Whitlam might have gone to the Palace to have Sir John Kerr sacked ... If the fear of Sir John Kerr was that he would lose his job, that was not a proper consideration. Soldiers die for the Crown every day and, therefore, he should not have taken that into account, in my view.[10]

In Kerr's own mind he and Prince Charles went way back—to at least the previous year, when Kerr had been blessed with a startlingly frank discussion about the Prince's endless wait to ascend to the throne, his royal *ennui,* a sort of privileged loose end that the Governor-General had been only too willing to help tie up.[11] This confidence was made during the Prince's 1974 Australian tour, when Kerr, who had been appointed Governor-General by Prime Minister Gough Whitlam just months earlier, also discussed with Prince Charles the suggestion that he might one day come to Australia as Governor-General.

It would have been, as Kerr wished it to be, a return to the quasi-colonial pre-war days of national deference and royal sinecure, with the viceroy an opportunistic posting for lesser royals and a safe haven for aristocratic embarrassments. The view of the Prime Minister, whose responsibility it was to determine and appoint the Governor-General, appears to have had no bearing on this remarkable vice-regal indiscretion. Whitlam would have been appalled by the breach of governmental protocol implicit in Kerr's presumption of a power to discuss the post and aghast at the suggestion of any royal re-entry into Australian civic life at a time when his government was determinedly removing the 'relics of colonialism' and arcane privilege.

Having failed in his efforts to mediate Prince Charles's interest in taking up the mantle of Governor-General, Kerr later suggested to Whitlam that the Australian government purchase a large rural holding with appropriate homestead, servants, upkeep and furnishings, to encourage the Prince of Wales to make more regular and longer trips to Australia. An astonished Whitlam declined, suggesting that the purchase of an Australian property for the use of the Prince of Wales was not a priority for national expenditure. In later private letters to Prince Charles, and with the most deferential and subordinate genuflection—'I have the honour to remain, Sir, your most loyal and obedient servant'—Kerr would refer to these conversations as lasting moments of treasured privilege: 'I have the very great privilege of remembering a number of conversations which you have been kind enough to have with me in past years'.[12]

From that time on Kerr was in constant and regular contact with the Palace, first through his discussions with Prince Charles and subsequently through his 'regular and thorough reporting to the Queen' from September 1975 and throughout the crisis. Through his 'conversations with the Queen and with Sir Martin Charteris', his letters to the Queen, to Charles, and more frequently to Charteris, Kerr maintained a steady recitation on the vicissitudes of the Whitlam government, in a vice-regal subverting of his Prime Minister and his government.[13] Kerr's journal, and his direct quotations in it from his correspondence with the Queen and with Charteris, show that the Palace was kept informed of his consideration of the dismissal of the Whitlam government months before there was even any 'political crisis' to report. Kerr had conveyed his thoughts about dismissing Whitlam and his resultant fears about his own job security to Charteris and, even earlier, to Prince Charles in New Guinea, as well as to the Queen.

There can be no doubt that, contrary to Kerr's claim and the popular view, Prince Charles, Sir Martin Charteris and the Queen were aware that the Governor-General was considering dismissing Gough Whitlam and that none of them had raised any concern—either about such a move or that Kerr was communicating directly with them on this. Most significantly, at no stage did the Palace inform the Prime Minister that the Governor-General was communicating with them in this way without Whitlam's knowledge or approval, and that he was considering such extreme unilateral action against him. Their failure to inform Whitlam, as Kerr himself should have done, could only have given Kerr tacit comfort and confidence that the dismissal of the Prime Minister would not meet any royal resistance.

Among Kerr's trove of previously unpublished private papers is a loose collection of 'miscellaneous handwritten notes', generic thoughts and key points on the dismissal, which Kerr revisited in his book *Matters for Judgment*. A rough list in Kerr's own hand, under the heading 'Dismissal', includes the following four points matching the trajectory of his contacts with the Palace during this time:

- New Guinea—Prince of Wales
- My relation with the Prince of Wales
- Prince's conversation with MC [Martin Charteris]
- Charteris's advice to me on dismissal.[14]

Not only was the Palace aware of the possibility of dismissal, the Queen's private secretary had himself provided 'advice' to the Governor-General. Yet all of those involved have continued steadfastly to deny that the Queen had *any* prior knowledge of Kerr's thinking or his intentions. As recently as 2011 Sir William Heseltine, the Queen's assistant private secretary at the time of the dismissal, stated that: 'The Governor-General *gave no clue* to any of us at the palace what was in his mind'.[15] *No clue?* Private conversations, personal letters, an agreement to delay his recall and 'Charteris's advice to me on dismissal'—these were more than just clues; this was advance knowledge of a well-advanced plan.

That Charteris's advice to Kerr on this contained no adverse comment about the prospect of the Governor-General dismissing his Prime Minister without warning, and established instead that the Queen would try to delay any advice from Whitlam to recall Kerr as Governor-General for as long as possible, can only be seen as an unqualified royal green light to Kerr's dismissal of Whitlam.

What should have happened is simple and uncontroversial. From the first time that the Governor-General raised the crisis and his consideration of even the possibility of dismissal, the Queen and her advisers should have asked him whether he had discussed it with the Prime Minister and should have reminded him of his fundamental responsibility to take the advice of his Prime Minister. Not that Kerr needed any reminding of this basic democratic relationship; he had described it himself just six months earlier in a speech at the Union Club in Sydney: 'Everyone knows that the Governor-General must act upon the advice of his ministers—his constitutional advisers'.[16] By failing to inform the Prime Minister of their discussions with Kerr and by failing to alert Whitlam to Kerr's canvassing of his dismissal, the Palace not only abetted Kerr's deception, it was complicit in it.

Kerr's own private papers have now shown the claim of monarchical ignorance of and insulation from the Governor-General's actions to be untrue, a historical fiction insistently circulated from the moment of Whitlam's dismissal and maintained for nearly forty years. Revelations from Kerr's papers first published in 2012 in *Gough Whitlam: His Time* and these continuing disclosures from them, conclusively dispel Kerr's claim to have acted in isolation and in response to an immediate and intractable crisis. They demonstrate instead that Kerr had kept informed a highly significant network of political, legal and royal contacts on the possibility of dismissal and of his concern for his own position, without the knowledge of the Prime Minister and in breach of his responsibility to him.

This was not the only revelation to come from the rather unsettling, obsessive reworkings of these events that litter Kerr's archives. Kerr's private papers in themselves constitute a remarkable turnaround, manifesting a concern for the posthumous righting of the historical record that he himself had so wilfully distorted. There was one person in particular whose identity Kerr was determined to reveal and whose role in the dismissal, Kerr wrote, should not remain 'in the shades of history'.

2

WHAT DID THE HIGH COURT JUSTICE(S) KNOW?

ON THE AFTERNOON of 9 November 1975 the Governor-General, Sir John Kerr, made a telephone call to the Chief Justice of the High Court of Australia, Sir Garfield Barwick. Kerr sought a meeting with Barwick the following day at Admiralty House in Sydney, to discuss his intention to dismiss Whitlam and to obtain Barwick's legal and written assurance that it was not only legal but, as Barwick described it, 'his constitutional duty' to do so.[1] In meeting Barwick and seeking his opinion Kerr was acting against the express advice of the Prime Minister, Gough Whitlam, who had told Kerr that he would not agree to their meeting. Whitlam was adamant that Kerr should not confer with the Chief Justice not only because the Governor-General's proper legal advisers were the Solicitor-General and the Attorney-General but also because in the recent tightly split High Court decisions relating to Whitlam government legislation, Barwick had ruled consistently with the minority against the government and, finally, because the High Court had decided in 1921 that it could not give advisory opinions. The Chief Justice moreover, while of obvious status, has no special constitutional position either in authority or weight of judgement. As Barwick himself put it, 'I have no authority at all as Chief Justice with respect to the other men [other justices]. I have none at all'.[2] His opinion therefore was of no greater standing than that of any other justice—Kerr might just as well have sought the advice of High Court Justice Lionel Murphy, with vastly different results.

Barwick agreed to meet Kerr on 10 November, on his way to the High Court sittings in Sydney. He requested that Kerr make their meetings public, insisting on an announcement in the Vice-Regal News column of the daily papers on 11 November 1975, and that his opinion be given to Kerr in writing.[3] Ignoring Whitlam's advice to Kerr that he not confer with Barwick, of which Barwick was also aware, Kerr and Barwick then discussed Kerr's decision to dismiss the Whitlam government, on which Barwick agreed to prepare written advice. Kerr also told Barwick that he was curious to know the view of High Court Justice Sir Anthony Mason, suggesting that Barwick might ask Mason for it. And so, after the morning sitting of the High Court, Barwick showed his draft advice to his fellow Justice, Mason, who 'quite agreed with the view I had expressed'.[4] Barwick then returned to Admiralty House for a second meeting with the Governor-General and the two conferred again over an elaborate lunch.

The following week, shocked by the scale of criticism he faced in the days after the dismissal, Kerr asked Barwick for permission to release his written advice and Barwick, reluctantly it appears, agreed.[5] With this concurrence Barwick would be forever tied to and tarred by the dismissal. His almost defiant insistence on public recognition would ensure his lasting notoriety as Kerr's accomplice, even to some his 'co-conspirator'. It was a mantle Garfield Barwick wore with pride. Barwick's curmudgeonly, unapologetic nature seemed to relish every reproach, and there were many, from among his own court to incredulous journalists baffled by his attempted yet surprisingly fragile justifications. To his fellow High Court justice, Lionel Murphy's furious rebuke, 'I dissociate myself completely from your action in advising the Governor-General and for the advice you gave', Barwick made no effort to hide his disdain: 'I note your remarks. I fundamentally disagree with them, both as to any legal opinion they involved and as to any matter of the propriety of my conduct. I see no need to discuss with you either question'. To a journalist inquiring what basis there was for Barwick's claim of a 'Constitutional duty' for Kerr's actions, 'What section of the Constitution lays down that the Governor-General's duty would be to commission the Opposition as a caretaker government?', Barwick replied defiantly and without a hint of self-doubt, 'None'. 'Which section is that again Sir Garfield?', he was asked in disbelief, 'I said, none!'.[6]

At the same time, Barwick further muddied the Constitutional waters by denying that, in dismissing Whitlam, Kerr had acted on the basis of the Governor-General's putative 'reserve powers': 'It isn't reserve power at all. It's a simple case of a Minister who can't provide the Crown with money for the ordinary services of the Government can't remain the Crown's Minister'.

Like Kerr, Barwick had acted just as he wanted to act, free of institutional, governmental or conventional constraint. But, unlike John Kerr, Garfield Barwick revealed no personal insecurity, no hesitation, and certainly no regret over those actions. Barwick's written advice to Kerr stated that the activation of this 'Constitutional duty' would follow *if* the Prime Minister refused 'to advise a general election or resign'—neither of which Whitlam had refused to do, since Kerr had not asked him. Yet Barwick remained completely unmoved and unrepentant when this disagreeable qualifier in his own advice to the Governor-General was pointed out to him later. Although Barwick stated that his advice to Kerr was a matter of law only—as if the removal of an elected government can be considered absent of politics—his actions clearly were not. Barwick's decision to meet Kerr despite Whitlam's advice to the contrary, and his decision to advise the Governor-General in contradiction to advice already received from the Solicitor-General and Attorney-General, were political decisions masquerading as law.

The dismissal immediately became seen as a tandem act, with Kerr and Barwick as the lead players and with Barwick even seen as the mastermind, the Svengali to Kerr's weak and pliable recreant. David Marr writes that as he began work on his biography of Barwick he had a single purpose: 'to pin on the man his responsibility for the crimes of 11 November 1975 ... to show how a great lawyer could bring himself to collaborate with Sir John Kerr in the downfall of an elected government'.[7]

That Barwick had indeed 'collaborated' then seemed beyond question.

From what we now know, however, this assessment is too harsh. Barwick came into Kerr's deliberations on the mechanics of the dismissal very late, after the letter of dismissal and the statement of reasons had been written, after months of secret communication with the Palace, and after Whitlam had informed Kerr that he was to hold a half-Senate election. Both Kerr and Barwick agree that on 10 November 1975 Barwick provided written advice on a path of action that had already been determined.[8] Yet Barwick was prepared, even willing, to take the full brunt of public opprobrium and historical judgement as the High Court 'collaborator' with the Governor-General on the dismissal of the Whitlam government.

There was, however, another story, one kept carefully and deliberately hidden from public view and the details of which are still surfacing today.

If this document is found among my archives, it will mean that my final decision is that truth must prevail, and, as he played a most significant part in my thinking at that critical time, and as he will be in the shades of history when this is read, his role should be known.

This file, which I unearthed among Kerr's private papers during archival research for *Gough Whitlam: His Time,* described the extensive and secret role of the then High Court Justice Sir Anthony Mason in the dismissal.[9] It has been described as 'a discovery of historical importance' and it is without doubt the most important material to emerge about the dismissal in four decades.[10] Kerr's file confirmed, after years of speculation, Mason's identity as the 'other authority' with whom Kerr had conferred about the dismissal; it revealed for the first time the previously unimagined extent of Mason's interactions with Kerr and involvement in the dismissal and, finally, it suggested that Barwick had been wrongly cast in history as the guiding force behind the wavering Governor-General.

Seven years after the dismissal, on the anniversary of that dramatic divisive day Barwick wrote to Kerr in a rare moment of reflection on their actions and on Mason's still secret involvement. Barwick also recalled their conversations with the 'younger man' who had been crucially involved in the dismissal of the Whitlam government, contemplating whether they should make his identity known or whether Barwick should continue to carry the burden of his historical role as the legal *bête noire* behind the dismissal: 'I feel strongly that the younger man should not be involved,' Barwick wrote. Kerr replied in qualified agreement:

> I feel with you that 'the younger man should not be involved'. I have no desire to bring forward Mason's name, certainly not at this stage, though I feel that it may be desirable, before the history is finally written, for it to be known what he actually believed, but not until after our deaths.[11]

Sir Anthony Mason himself remained silent.

The history of course had by that time already been written, and it had been written with this one glaring error—the absence of Mason. This exchange of letters between Kerr and Barwick seven years after the dismissal, shows their shared determination to keep Mason's involvement secret, a deliberately constructed history which they undertook to maintain for as long as they deemed it necessary. Kerr and Barwick agreed to keep Mason's role—of which Barwick knew little—from public and historical view in order to protect Sir Anthony Mason, then a rising figure on the High Court bench, from the continuing condemnation that they themselves had faced for their actions in dismissing Whitlam.

In the early rush of books exploring these unprecedented events, marked by a determination to understand the complexities of Kerr's interactions with Fraser, with the Palace and with the High Court, Sir Anthony Mason barely rated a mention. On those rare occasions that his name was raised, Mason was considered merely a bit player in the drama played out by the Governor-General and his 'collaborator', the Chief Justice, Sir Garfield Barwick.

As the historical record took shape, this most significant flaw remained largely unchallenged, despite the occasional breakouts suggesting that Mason had in some way been involved. Rumours that Kerr's actions had involved someone other than Sir Garfield Barwick had begun with the release of Kerr's memoirs, *Matters for Judgment,* in which he referred to 'conversation with one person only other than the Chief Justice', a conversation that Kerr states did not include advice, before the dismissal.[12] This was later identified as a reference to Mason, whose role was at that stage still seen as relatively minor, as that of 'the third man'—the sidekick to the two main players, Kerr and Barwick.[13]

While Barwick's apologia *Sir John Did His Duty* makes no mention of Mason's involvement, his autobiography, written twelve years later, does. A new element in the history of the dismissal was now slowly taking shape, as Barwick acknowledged that he had shown his written advice to the Governor-General to Mason, his fellow Justice, at the suggestion of Kerr.

Barwick recounts that during Kerr's telephone call late on 9 November 1975 to arrange their meeting the following day, Kerr had also suggested that Barwick might seek Mason's view. Unknown to Barwick, Mason was with Kerr when this telephone call, and this suggestion, was made. Barwick did as Kerr suggested and sought Mason out and, not surprisingly in this round-robin of judicial corroboration, was pleased to report that, 'He said he quite agreed with the view I had expressed'.[14] Like so much of the history of the dismissal, Mason's role was emerging only fitfully and even then, twenty years after the dismissal, the extent of his involvement was not yet clear. Mason had refused requests to be interviewed and declined to make a statement, and so, his full role remained unknown.[15]

And there the history stalled, controlled and constructed by all parties, with Mason playing a gradually unfolding but still uncertain role. It was not until the publication of Kerr's own record of their extensive interactions thirty-seven years later that Mason's role in the dismissal was known. These revelations, published in *Gough Whitlam: His Time,* definitively show Mason to have been the long-term legal eminence behind the Governor-General, guiding his thinking, his deliberations and, in Kerr's words, 'fortifying me for the action I was to take'.

It had been a willing subterfuge in which Kerr and Barwick retained control of the agreed history, directing a narrative that pointed always to Barwick as Kerr's High Court connection and deflecting attention from the other key player in the dismissal, whose identity both Kerr and Barwick were committed to protecting. Together they had determined on what was in effect another conspiracy, a conspiracy against history, to allow an incomplete historical record to take shape and to hide from the public the full story, the identity and the role of the then High Court Justice Sir Anthony Mason. Mason's role was extensive; it stretched back many months, long before Kerr contacted Sir Garfield Barwick for his opinion, months before there was a Supply crisis to discuss and continuing even in the hours after the dismissal as parliament resumed sitting for the afternoon session of 11 November 1975. Yet, despite his now undoubted significance, Mason was lost to history for nearly four decades, until the discovery of Kerr's dramatic record of their interactions.

What we now know is that several months before the Opposition first refused to allow a vote in the Senate on the Supply bills, Kerr sought a legal and academic buffer for his sweeping view of the Governor-General's discretionary powers and what those powers might enable him to do. Kerr had been Governor-General for barely four months when he first sought the help of his long-term friend Sir Anthony Mason in forming a highly confidential advisory group of senior members of the Australian National University Law School, to advise him on the nature and extent of his vice-regal powers. It was an utterly inexplicable and professionally humiliating scenario—the Governor-General, an immediate past Chief Justice of the Supreme Court of New South Wales, needing and seeking career advice.

Once the advisory group had been set up, Mason withdrew, in language that shows he was aware of the concerns that might be raised by the existence of this group within the university and his involvement, as a High Court justice, in it: 'I doubt whether it would be proper for me to become a member of the group on a continuing basis', he told Kerr. The senior staff at the ANU law school maintained their confidentiality, although privately some mocked 'the Governor-General's tutorials' as if Kerr was an undergraduate in need of remedial assistance. In the end Professor Geoffrey Sawer heeded the 'alarm bells' that the university was involving itself in matters of intense contemporary political controversy and the Governor-General's tutorials ceased.

From this point on Mason's personal role as confidant and counsel for Kerr intensified, with a series of clandestine conversations between the Governor-General and the High Court Justice beginning in August. Whitlam was never informed of these meetings and they were not reported in the

Vice-Regal News. In seeking Mason's counsel Kerr was acting in defiance of the fundamental expectation that the Governor-General act on the advice of his ministers, and on the legal advice of the chief law officers, the Solicitor-General and the Attorney-General. Over the course of these three months, Kerr and Mason canvassed the political situation and the increasing tension in the Senate and, as opposition Senators moved to block the government's budget bills, they considered the role to be played by the Governor-General in determining the fate of the Whitlam government. Most remarkably and most disturbingly, Kerr and Mason discussed the timing and the means through which the Governor-General could dismiss Whitlam as Prime Minister, and install the Leader of the Opposition, Fraser, as Prime Minister in his place.

The publication of Kerr's archival record in 2012 in *Gough Whitlam: His Time* also succeeded in drawing out a very reluctant Mason to make his first and only public statement on the dismissal. After decades of silence

Mason now acknowledged his role, confirming the substance of Kerr's record in a written statement that added to what was still, even then, an incomplete history. In his version of these long-hidden interactions, Mason revealed that he had strongly urged Kerr not to take this unprecedented step of dismissal without first warning Whitlam; 'I told him that, if he did not warn the prime minister, he would run the risk that people would accuse him of being deceptive', and that he had cautioned Kerr that dismissal without warning was 'bound to attract strong criticism'. Mason claimed to have insisted to Kerr that 'as a matter of fairness' Whitlam should be given the option of calling a general election as Prime Minister, rather than face outright dismissal without warning. This is a major point of difference between Kerr and Mason's versions of events that is yet to be resolved, since Mason has declined to be interviewed about the dismissal.[16] Kerr's record makes no mention of Mason's caution to him that he ought first to warn Whitlam, to speak to him about his options and to lay bare Kerr's intended actions should Whitlam not accede to them. This is precisely what Kerr had refused to do, citing his concern for his own position—that he himself might be dismissed—in dismissing Whitlam without warning.

Mason also revealed one of the most significant aspects of his involvement in the dismissal—that he had drafted a letter dismissing Whitlam for the Governor-General. Although Mason states that his draft letter of dismissal was not used by Kerr, this is hardly the salient point. The fact is, from Mason's own words, he drafted a letter dismissing Whitlam for the Governor-General, some days before the dismissal took place. From his own statement then it is clear that Mason was aware of the pending dismissal, he counselled Kerr on it, he conferred with him about the wording of the letter of dismissal and he met Kerr in secret and against Whitlam's express advice to the Governor-General that any meetings with third parties were to be agreed to by him. Mason's involvement in the dismissal is beyond doubt and his concealing of it from history a dereliction. Mason has continued to decline requests to release his draft letter of dismissal, not even for the benefit of the historical record. 'I owe history nothing' was his astonishing response to my question about this.

Whitlam, and history, was not the only one deceived in this carefully crafted narrative in which Mason's involvement in the dismissal was successfully airbrushed from public view for so long. It now appears that Chief Justice Barwick was also deceived, for in their final deliberations Mason and Kerr discussed at what point they should bring the Chief Justice into their planning, to garner Barwick's legal imprimatur in support of the dismissal of Whitlam. Kerr's archival record suggests that Barwick knew nothing of these meetings between Mason and Kerr in the months leading up to Barwick's opinion being sought. Barwick was equally unaware that his fellow High Court Justice, Sir Anthony Mason, was with Kerr when the Governor-General telephoned seeking an appointment with him for 10 November 1975.

Barwick's historically presumed role as Kerr's legal éminence grise in the dismissal deserves reassessment. The revelations of the extensive role played by Mason also cast doubt on the role long accorded to Barwick as the driving force—the 'mastermind' in Kerr's words, the 'plug' in Barwick's own description—behind the vacillating Kerr.[17] From what we now know this is a term and a role more appropriately applied to Mason.

The impropriety in Kerr conferring with Mason in this way is at once personal in its deception, and political in its defiance of the Prime Minister's advice and its complication of the separation of powers. Kerr should have done exactly as he had previously acknowledged he should do—acted on the advice of his ministers. By October, Whitlam had reminded Kerr of this fundamental equation most firmly when the Governor-General had first asked whether he might confer with the Chief Justice. Whitlam told Kerr he should speak to the Attorney-General and, with Whitlam's approval, the Solicitor-General on legal matters. This was not, as Kerr chose to portray it, intended as a personal affront, it was a straightforward statement of the political relationship between them. As Governor-General, Kerr was an appointed official, his role was defined by his formal relationship to the head of elected government—the Prime Minister.

The revelations of Kerr's extensive interactions with Mason and of Mason's role in the dismissal, coming decades later, are also a powerful reminder that, no matter how much has been written or how definitive the consensus appears to be, so much can still remain forgotten, hidden or simply wrong. For the history of the dismissal of the Whitlam government has been not only a forgotten history, but also a deliberately and deceptively hidden one.

3

WHAT DID MALCOLM FRASER KNOW?

AS THE GOVERNOR-GENERAL'S appointed Prime Minister, Malcolm Fraser faced two persistent questions as news of the dismissal spread: first, did he have any prior knowledge that the Governor-General would dismiss Gough Whitlam? And second, did he have any private, unauthorised, discussions with the Governor-General in the weeks before the dismissal? On both these questions Fraser and Kerr were at one. Their denials were vehement and unwavering: Kerr had given Fraser no prior warning of the dismissal, and Fraser had had no discussions with Kerr prior to the dismissal other than those approved by the Prime Minister, Gough Whitlam.

Within hours of the dismissal, both Kerr and Fraser were forced to confront these swirling rumours; given the severity of their implications they were impossible to avoid. On the afternoon of 11 November, the Governor-General 'emphatically denied' that the Leader of the Opposition had any advance knowledge of his intention to dismiss Whitlam. Fraser told a rowdy press conference in Parliament House, his first as Prime Minister, that it was 'complete nonsense' to suggest that he had any prior knowledge, and that he had known nothing of Kerr's decision until after Whitlam had been dismissed.[1]

Having established these twin pillars of the historical record within hours of the dismissal, both Fraser and Kerr adhered to them for the next decade. It was a calculated fabrication, designed for self-preservation and a fundamental breach of public trust.

Fraser's repeated denials of any forewarning of the dismissal fell apart a decade later with his erstwhile colleague Senator Reg Withers's piqued revelation of the details of the Governor-General's telephone call to the Leader of the Opposition on the morning of 11 November 1975. Barely three years after the dismissal of the Whitlam government the man Gough Whitlam called 'Western Australia's gift to the arts of political chicanery', Reg Withers, was himself dismissed as Minister for Administrative Services by Fraser, following a Royal Commission finding of impropriety against him in relation to an electoral redistribution. A furious, spurned and increasingly bitter Withers retorted, 'When the man who's carried the biggest knife in this country for the last ten years starts giving you a lecture about propriety, integrity and the need to resign, then he's either making a sick joke or playing you for a mug'.[2] Reg Withers was no mug; he bided his time before dropping the sensational claim that Kerr and Fraser had discussed the terms of Fraser's appointment as Prime Minister *before* Kerr dismissed Whitlam and not, as both Fraser and Kerr had previously insisted, after.

As Withers' remarks became known Fraser soon capitulated, recasting his previous denials and now acknowledging that Kerr had indeed put to him before the dismissal four conditions on which the Governor-General would appoint him Prime Minister. According to Fraser, who detailed these to his biographer Philip Ayres in 1987, the key undertakings were to:

- Guarantee Supply;
- Immediately recommend a double dissolution;
- Undertake no new policies and make no appointments of significance before an election;
- Initiate no inquiries into the activities and policies of the Whitlam Government.[3]

But even this reluctant confessional was not entirely accurate. It would only later become clear that the fourth of these undertakings was not a general embargo against any future inquiries into the actions of the previous government—a reasonable and appropriate expectation for any government—but a specific undertaking by Malcolm Fraser not to hold a Royal Commission into the Executive Council meeting of 14 December 1975—the 'loans affair'. A note of this vital conversation made by Fraser's private secretary at the time and subsequently released reads simply; '4. No Royal Commission'.[4] As Leader of the

Opposition, Fraser had been pushing for a Royal Commission into the 'loans affair' for several months. In early July 1975, the Attorney-General's department had advised the government of the 'distinct possibility' that the Opposition would establish a Committee of Inquiry in the Senate if the government did not establish a Royal Commission itself.[5] Yet Kerr was now insisting that Fraser reverse his position on this, as a condition of forming government.

Fraser's own memoirs describe it as 'a less expected and highly significant' undertaking that the Governor-General was asking the Leader of the Opposition to agree to in order to be appointed to government.[6] It was 'less expected' because with this condition, the Governor-General was requiring a specific policy reversal be agreed to before appointing the Leader of the Opposition as Prime Minister. It was 'highly significant', and clearly improper, because this was a policy matter that directly involved Kerr himself.

There was a perfect irony in this unveiling of an agreed historical fiction coming from Reg Withers. Many considered Withers to be the architect of this political Ponzi scheme—the Opposition using its numbers in the Senate to remove the government formed in the House of Representatives. Withers, like many of his conservative colleagues who had not seen Opposition for twenty-three years, harboured a particular disdain for the democratic process that had so presumptuously delivered this unwanted verdict, describing the election of the Whitlam government in December 1972 as an 'aberration', the result of the 'temporary electoral insanity' of the electorate.[7] Those views, and the longstanding political and bureaucratic expectations, habits and networks they reflected, lay at the heart of the sense of illegitimacy that swirled around the Whitlam government from the moment of its inception. Despite the re-election of the Whitlam government in May 1974 this denial of legitimacy only escalated.

Although roundly denied at the time, senior members of the Opposition were also in contact with the Governor-General prior to the dismissal. In 1979 former Liberal Prime Minister

Billy McMahon acknowledged for the first time that he had communicated with Kerr *before* 11 November about the possibility of Whitlam's dismissal. McMahon's view, which he had conveyed strongly to Kerr, was that the Governor-General had 'neither the power nor the Constitutional right' to dismiss Whitlam. 'He didn't take any notice of me, regrettably', McMahon said ruefully.[8] McMahon recalled that he had 'informed' Kerr of his opinion and that Kerr had 'acknowledged receipt' of it, suggesting that their contact had been in writing rather than in person. Shortly before the dismissal McMahon had asked his private secretary, Robert Ashley, to personally deliver an envelope to Government House—an unusual task that would normally be undertaken by his driver. Ashley drove to Yarralumla, where he was met at the gatehouse by the Governor-General's official secretary, David Smith, who was expecting him and the envelope. Ashley has suggested that the document was 'possibly mediating the opinion of one of his [McMahon's] senior learned friends'.[9]

McMahon disagreed vehemently with Kerr's action in dismissing Whitlam without warning, later describing it as having brought parliament into greatest disrepute. McMahon's concern was the 'loans affair' and he pursued it relentlessly, in and out of government.[10]

On 10 November 1975 the Liberal Party of Australia received a formal legal opinion on the Executive Council meeting of 14 December 1974 from veteran Sydney barrister Alec Shand QC. This was the Executive Council meeting, attended by Whitlam, Lionel Murphy, Jim Cairns and Rex Connor, at which the international search for loans 'for temporary purposes' in order to fund the major energy infrastructure projects of the Minister for Energy Rex Connor's 'magnificent obsession'—the northwest shelf pipeline and publicly owned energy exploration, production and distribution to the south-eastern states—had been approved. Among his claims of illegality, deceit and bad faith on the part of the four Whitlam government ministers in their representations to the Executive Council,

Shand also considered the possible inclusion of the Governor-General, Sir John Kerr in any prospective charges of fraud and illegality. One of the questions to be considered, Shand wrote, 'is the legality or lawfulness ... of the decisions taken by the Governor-General in Council'.[11] It was Kerr whose signature, as Governor-General, had formally authorised the Minutes of that meeting and although, Shand noted, he was not 'aware of any evidence which would justify' including Kerr in 'the allegation of deceit relating to these executive decisions', he did not close this possibility off. Merely by raising this prospect, Shand had placed Kerr clearly in the mix of future charges against the four ministers for which, Shand advised, there was 'ample justification'.[12]

On any reading this was a devastating prospect for the Governor-General. Fraser had in the previous months been demanding a Royal Commission into precisely these matters, an inquiry that would inevitably involve Kerr since his authorisation as Governor-General of the Executive

Council Minute in December 1974 had enabled the 'loans affair' to proceed. Kerr's archival records and personal commentaries reveal his grievous fear at this prospect. Fraser understood Kerr's fears precisely. Kerr had told others that Fraser was, 'threatening ... to denounce him as a Labor party stooge', and Fraser himself described the 'immense pressure' he was putting on the Governor-General to act.[13] At their last publicly reported meeting on 6 November Fraser spoke exceptionally forcefully to the Governor-General, telling Kerr that 'if there's not an election ... I'm going to have to say something about what that means, it will mean obviously saying something about this office ... he [Kerr] would not want to be condemned for failing the office'. Fraser made it clear that the authorisation of the Executive Council minute by the Governor-General would be part of that condemnation.[14] In his previously unpublished interview for the National Library with Clyde Cameron, Fraser recounts that he spoke even more strongly to Kerr at this last meeting, telling him that if an election was not called, 'I will have to say how you have failed in your duty to the Australian people and to the Australian Constitution'.[15] For the Leader of the Opposition to speak in such brutal, threatening terms to the Governor-General was an unthinkable breach of political and institutional protocol and of personal respect.

Kerr was already deeply concerned by criticism of him in relation to his authorisation of the Minute, criticism he claimed indicated a 'lack of knowledge in the community about what had happened'. The Governor-General was particularly pained by criticism that, 'I had apparently preferred to be at the Opera than at a very important Executive Council meeting'.[16] Laurie Oakes reported Kerr's immense discomfort at the sniping from his legal brethren: 'Could you let me have a few billion dollars for temporary purposes, John?'.[17] If Kerr feared anything more than his own recall as Governor-General by Whitlam, it was the personal and professional humiliation of being called before an inquiry in relation to the 'loans affair'. Shand's legal opinion is dated 10 November 1975. The following morning Kerr contacted Fraser and put to him the terms on which he would agree to appoint Fraser Prime Minister, the fourth of these being that there would be no Royal Commission into the Executive Council meeting of 14 December 1974. Fraser agreed at once.

Fraser and Kerr always maintained that their only contact throughout the weeks leading up to 11 November 1975 was at official, authorised meetings, each of which took place with Whitlam's knowledge and approval. Despite lingering suspicions that the two men were in contact unknown to Whitlam, Kerr and Fraser repeatedly denied this. 'Nothing could have been farther from the truth ... The story was false and ridiculous', Kerr wrote in his memoirs, '[n]othing whatever passed between Mr Fraser and myself, directly or indirectly, except what is recorded in this book'.[18] Fraser was insistent on this also and his later memoirs refer only to his approved meetings with Kerr: 'There was no secret about it; Fraser had sought Whitlam's permission, which had been willingly given'.[19] No other contact with the Governor-General is mentioned.

We owe it once again to the disgruntled Reg Withers that this historical falsity has now been exposed. Soon after his own dismissal from the Fraser ministry, Withers gave off-the-record briefings in which he claimed that Kerr and Fraser had several unreported personal telephone conversations during the month leading up to the dismissal.[20] Withers at this stage provided no further information about these claimed secret communications between the Governor-General and the Leader of the Opposition, which had long been rumoured.[21]

Withers saved the most explosive claim to last, leaving a posthumous record of his knowledge of these private communications between Fraser and Kerr in the weeks before the dismissal. In a previously unpublished interview conducted two decades after the dismissal and embargoed until after his death, Withers finally corrects one of the enduring fictions in the history of the dismissal of the Whitlam government.[22]

Withers reveals that not only had Kerr decided to act against Whitlam in the week before 11 November 1975, but that both he and Fraser knew this. Withers confirms that the Governor-General and the Leader of the Opposition were in secret telephone contact, using their secure private numbers. Withers recounts that he was in Fraser's office in early November when Kerr contacted Fraser, using the private number for the Leader of the Opposition's parliamentary office. 'Nobody knew what his private number was except Tamie [Fraser's wife, Tamara]', Withers said. Fraser told the caller that he could be contacted on that number at any time and assured him that he would be the only person who would answer. Fraser then asked the caller for their number, repeating it as he wrote it down, 'I can also ring you on this number?' he asked. As Fraser wrote it down Withers also made a note of the number and later checked it. It was a Yarralumla prefix. The telephone call was short and as Fraser hung up he said to Withers, 'You never heard that conversation'. 'I never heard anything', Withers replied.

This secret communication between the Governor-General and the Leader of the Opposition is the most serious possible breach of the fundamental constitutional and political relationship that the Governor-General acts on the advice of the Prime Minister, not on that of the Leader of the Opposition. Their undisclosed contact reflects a complete breakdown in this formal relationship and an irredeemable breach of the processes of government.

Parliamentary governance simply could not function and in 1975 it did not function, with the Governor-General working against both convention and constitutional requirement by remaining 'silent' to the Prime Minister while secretly conferring with the Leader of the Opposition against the advice and the knowledge of the Prime Minister. Had these interactions been known at the time they occurred, it would have spelt the certain political end for both Kerr and Fraser; neither could have continued in their respective office had there been any broader knowledge of their secret dealings, the substance of those interactions and the casuistry of the denials to follow.

Kerr had assured Whitlam that he would meet the Leader of the Opposition only with Whitlam's approval and full knowledge. By secretly contacting Fraser, during the most divisive episode in our political history, Kerr had crossed the lines of political propriety, personal integrity and professional disinterest—he had become a partisan figure.

Equally shocking is that in the history of the dismissal, in the thousands of words written and spoken and passionately debated about it, the false trail so carefully established and tended by Kerr and Fraser was rarely questioned. The twin pillars of what had become known simply as 'the dismissal' were, it now appears, entirely false.

4

AMBUSH: THE HALF-SENATE ELECTION

IT IS ALMOST impossible for us to imagine this today, but when Gough Whitlam arrived at Parliament House early on 11 November 1975, he believed that the parliamentary crisis was over. Five days earlier he had reached the decision that he had kept in reserve since the Opposition Senators had first refused to vote on Supply, to call a half-Senate election. The half-Senate election was due any time before 30 June 1976 and, as Prime Minister, it was Whitlam's sole prerogative to determine the date on which to call it.

The Governor-General Sir John Kerr was well aware that the decision to call the half-Senate election had been made, since Whitlam had informed him of it shortly before an Executive Council meeting on 6 November. Kerr raised no concerns. As protocol directed, and as Whitlam insisted, the paperwork had then been sent to Kerr at Yarralumla on 7 November 1975—four days before the dismissal. Again, Kerr raised no concerns. The Governor-General had even been sent a copy of the draft of Whitlam's formal letter advising the half-Senate election—it arrived while he was still in Sydney, attending to his secret meetings with Mason and Barwick. Again, Kerr raised no concerns. There can be no question that all of these key players knew that the 'crisis' had ended, nor that the Governor-General had been informed of it. Responsible government simply cannot function if the Prime Minister, on notifying the Governor-General of such a momentous decision, on sending him the draft documents and finalising the election date with him, can later be told by the Governor-General that the half-Senate election had not been agreed to. It was a ludicrous sophistry.

Kerr had agreed to a further meeting with Whitlam on 11 November at Yarralumla, at which the Prime

Minister would deliver the formal letter advising the half-Senate election that he had first confirmed with the Governor-General nearly a week earlier. A copy of Whitlam's detailed advice can be found in the National Archives, inscribed by hand, *'but the recommendation was not made'.* Whitlam had intended, following the agreed exchange of documents relating to the half-Senate election, to announce the election in the Parliament on the afternoon of 11 November 1975.

In all these discussions about the half-Senate election, the Governor-General had raised no concerns with Whitlam about this course of action, much less suggested that he would refuse to accept the Prime Minister's advice. And nor could he, for the decision to call the half-Senate election was entirely the Prime Minister's to make. This is the source of Whitlam's insistent grievance that he was 'ambushed' by Kerr on 11 November 1975, lured to Yarralumla apparently to finalise the paperwork for a half-Senate election that Kerr himself had accepted days earlier. Kerr later acknowledged the artifice: 'Whitlam had every reason to believe I was trying to get a late Senate election.'[1] The reality was, Kerr had spent those five days finalising the details not of the half-Senate election but of Whitlam's dismissal.

Kerr's own notes from his private papers reveal this deception to be a deliberate and calculated disarming of the Prime Minister through a strategic use of 'silence', of 'stealth', justified by Kerr's claims of what Whitlam *might* do and by Kerr's increasingly bizarre attempts to psycho-pathologise Whitlam: 'the Prime Minister was not entitled to know the steps in my thinking ... because he was not open to reason'; Whitlam was a 'dictator' who 'was waging psychological warfare against me'. 'It would have been positively dangerous for me to try to open up unwelcome discussion with him', Kerr later wrote to Barwick.[2]

Whitlam had laid out his strategy, of pushing the Senate to vote on Supply before ultimately bringing forward the half-Senate election, to a caucus meeting immediately after Supply was first blocked. In several interviews over the following week Whitlam had repeated this fundamental stance: 'There has to be a half-Senate election before the end of the year, but I have not decided when I will recommend the Governor-General to ask the State Governments to issue writs'.[3] A departmental paper had considered the possibility of the half-Senate election from early October and the draft papers were progressively updated with new dates and timelines set throughout the course of the crisis.[4] It was an established and recognised option, the government's major strategic pressure point, and the outcome on which Whitlam had finally resolved. It was also the one outcome the Opposition feared most.

The Coalition's dread lay not only in the slight chance that the Whitlam government would gain temporary control of the Senate but that in doing so it would be in a position to pass its legislation implementing 'one vote one value', to equalise electorates. This prospect of electoral equity was particularly alarming for the National Country party which feared an electoral wipe-out from the redistribution of its numerous sparsely populated electorates—a 'rural gerrymander' that had artificially bolstered their numbers for decades. Whitlam said just days before the dismissal, 'they are prepared to go to any lengths to prevent a half-Senate election'.[5]

Only Whitlam's infuriating and implacable sense of institutional propriety had prevented him from announcing his decision to hold the half-Senate election to the House of Representatives or to the media before his appointment with Kerr at 1pm. Had this news been confirmed by Whitlam that morning, the Opposition Senators would have passed the budget, as Fraser has since acknowledged. This had been precisely the circumstance in 1974 when then Governor-General Sir Paul Hasluck agreed to Whitlam's request for a double dissolution election, subject to Whitlam obtaining Supply—which the Senate had then promptly passed. Whitlam and his senior government colleagues met Fraser and their Coalition counterparts at 9.30am on 11 November. In an unexpected compromise, Whitlam offered to delay the half-Senate election for at least six months, alleviating the Opposition's concern that the government might gain temporary control of the Senate. To Whitlam's surprise, Fraser was not prepared to even discuss it. Whitlam told the Opposition leadership group that the half-Senate election was to be announced later that day, that it was to be held on 13 December, and that he was shortly to see the Governor-General to exchange the formal documentation. Both leaders then left for their respective party meetings.

Like Kerr, Fraser dealt with the prospect of internal revolt quite easily, with silence—at the joint parties meeting later that morning he simply kept Whitlam's decision to call the half-Senate election from his own wavering members. Or, in the more forgiving words of his biographer Philip Ayres, Fraser 'neglected to say anything about Whitlam's decision to call a half-Senate election'.[6] Journalists eagerly waiting outside the joint parties meeting room for their comments on the decision were incredulous at what they took to be an Opposition caught entirely off-guard by this political resolution of the crisis; 'Fraser's been too scared to tell them' was the widespread view.[7]

The half-Senate election was the one outcome that Fraser and the Liberal/National Country party hierarchy were determined to avoid, for two reasons. First, the unique algebra of the Senate configuration in November 1975, with two replacement Senate seats to be filled by election together with two new Senators in each of the Northern Territory and ACT, presented the slim possibility that the Whitlam government could gain control of the Senate for six months, until the new Senators took their places in July 1976.[8] As if this were not bad enough, Malcolm Fraser also knew that if the half-Senate election was called, his Senators would pass Supply; 'what we would have done is to let Supply through in those circumstances'.[9] Other Coalition party members have also confirmed that faced with a half-Senate election, the Opposition senators would have passed Supply. Or, as Whitlam later put it, quoting Withers, 'The Opposition in the Senate was about to "melt away like snow in the desert". Only the intervention of the Governor-General acting politically, acting as a partisan, prevented that inevitable victory.'[10]

There is no doubt that the half-Senate election was the resolution of the deadlock in the Senate over Supply that Kerr had claimed he was seeking to resolve. That the half-Senate election would be both a resolution of the crisis and a successful outcome for Whitlam was so clear to Fraser that, in consultation with his senior colleagues, he had already established a contingency plan—as soon as Kerr announced the half-Senate election, Fraser would immediately call a party meeting and resign as leader.[11] But Fraser also knew that this was a step he would never have to take. As Whitlam and Fraser left the meeting of senior government and Opposition leaders at 10am on 11 November 1975, Fraser had asked Whitlam not to announce his decision to call the half-Senate election to the media. Too energised by the resolution at hand and with his mind turning to the election, Whitlam scarcely gave Fraser's request a second thought, agreeing at once. Only wily veteran Labor member Frank Crean, puzzled and streetwise, was concerned by Fraser's desire for secrecy.

Once Whitlam had informed the Labor party caucus of the half-Senate election later that morning (and with his customary deference to protocol he had requested the Governor-General's permission before doing so), the news soon spread through the press gallery. An immediate sense of relief that the 'crisis' had been resolved politically was obvious to the politicians, journalists and public servants who had been part of the precipitous events of the last month. As parliament resumed for the morning session at 11.45am, exhausted and exhilarated government members were strangely on edge, just waiting for the drama that would begin with the Prime Minister's announcement of the half-Senate election later that day. At midday the Canberra radio news bulletins reported that a half-Senate election was to be held on 13 December and as parliament rose for lunch at

12.55pm on 11 November 1975 planning for the election was well underway. The crisis in the Senate was already history.[12]

As soon as the House of Representatives adjourned for lunch, Whitlam went directly to his office, collected the letter to the Governor-General advising the half-Senate election, put it in his top pocket and left for Yarralumla. Barely fifteen minutes later the now dismissed Gough Whitlam arrived at the Lodge, as Leader of the Opposition, and sat down to a large steak. He had already rung his wife Margaret, who was then in Sydney, and her feisty words were ringing in his ears, 'He can't sack you, you're the Prime Minister. You should have slapped his face and told him to pull himself together!'[13]

Whitlam's decision to hold the half-Senate election is a crucial element, perhaps *the* crucial element, in the forgotten history of the dismissal. It is impossible to understand the reasons for and the timing of the dismissal without considering that simple fact of Whitlam's decision to call forward the half-Senate election. Yet despite its critical importance, for all the thousands of words written about the dismissal the decision to call the half-Senate election is rarely considered as the definitive action that it was, and few acknowledge that Whitlam had reached this decision and had informed Kerr of it several days earlier. Ayres suggests that Whitlam did not signal his decision to Kerr until the morning of 11 November 1975, while Oakes puts it at the afternoon of 10 November, describing Whitlam as having lost his enthusiasm for the half-Senate election throughout the course of the crisis.[14] Political journalist Paul Kelly is one of the few to have acknowledged that Whitlam's plans to call the election were well advanced and that the Governor-General was clearly aware of them.[15] Barwick for his part omits any mention, either of the half-Senate election as an option or Whitlam's decision to call it, claiming that Kerr had been forced to act because Whitlam had 'refused to resign or to advise the Governor-General to dissolve the Parliament or the House of Representatives'.[16] Barwick presents these as if they were Whitlam's only options. In many of the later discussions of the dismissal, the half-Senate election all but disappears, its place in history receding with time.[17]

The historical rewriting began with Kerr's 'Statement of Reasons' released after the dismissal and which, in all its four pages of justification and selective annotation, refers to the half-Senate election almost as an afterthought. Kerr describes the half-Senate election merely as a 'possibility' that 'might be held'. He wrote:

There has been discussion of the possibility that a half-Senate election might be held under circumstances in which the government has not obtained supply. If such advice were given to me I should feel constrained to reject it because a half-Senate election held whilst supply continues to be denied does not guarantee a prompt or sufficiently clear prospect of the deadlock being resolved.[18]

Kerr does not mention that the decision to hold the half-Senate election had been reached by Whitlam days earlier—in fact he does not mention Whitlam at all in relation to these half-Senate election discussions. However, a draft of this statement shows that Kerr had, literally, rewritten history. It reads; 'Mr Whitlam, whilst asserting his right to govern without supply, advised a half-Senate election. I felt constrained to reject this advice'. The draft makes it clear that Whitlam had advised Kerr of the half-Senate election, that Kerr had rejected it and, worse, that Kerr elected to misrepresent this critical fact in his final statement.[19] Kerr's oblique 'there has been discussion' suggests that the half-Senate election had remained hypothetical, not the final and conclusive decision of the Prime Minister and the resolution of the deadlock that, Kerr claims, had warranted dismissal. Second, Kerr presents his own predictive imagination as fact—for on what basis could he state so definitively that Supply would 'continue to be denied' *once the half-Senate election had been called?*

This is not a moot point, for Kerr's predecessor, Sir Paul Hasluck, had faced precisely this question just the previous year, following Whitlam's request for a double dissolution in the face of the Senate threatening to block Supply. Hasluck's response could not have been more different from Kerr's and what is quite intriguing is how little this previous example was called upon to provide some guidance—either to Kerr in his deliberations or in subsequent analyses of the dismissal. In April 1974, in circumstances that provide the closest precedent for the events of 1975, Governor-General Hasluck had dealt very differently—more effectively and with negligible political upheaval—with the situation of a threatened refusal of Supply. A comparative examination of the 1974 threat to block Supply would have shown not only what had previously been done but also, and more importantly, what Sir John Kerr *should* have done on 11 November 1975.

Just eighteen months earlier, the Opposition leader, Billy Snedden, had led his party over an electoral cliff with the decision to move to refuse a vote on the Whitlam government's Supply bills in the Senate. The Opposition at that time had a majority in the Senate of five, the Senate not having faced the voters at the 1972 election, and on 10 April 1974 the Opposition leader in the Senate, Reg Withers, proposed an amendment that the budget bills would not be considered until the government 'agrees to submit itself to the Australian people'. This amendment was never actually put. Whitlam had already determined that this unprecedented threat of the ultimate Senate obstruction would provide the best opportunity for the government to go to a double dissolution election, using the continued obstruction of its program in the Senate as its strongest electoral suit.

Whitlam then called on the Governor-General Sir Paul Hasluck, who accepted the Prime Minister's advice to hold the double dissolution. Given the threat to Supply in the Senate, however, Hasluck astutely granted the double dissolution with the significant proviso that it be conditional on the provision of Supply. The government leader in the Senate, Senator Lionel Murphy, announced the news to the

Senate that the election had been granted 'on condition that a definite assurance was given that the financial position was such that adequate provision could be made for carrying on the Public Service during the period of time covered by the elections'.[20] The Opposition, which had just that afternoon made the unprecedented threat to refuse a vote on the government's Supply bills, then passed Supply later that night. This was the precursor to the Whitlam government's second election victory, on 18 May 1974, at which Whitlam became the first Labor leader to win government at successive elections and the Labor party picked up three Senate seats, leaving it equal with the Coalition on twenty-nine seats apiece—the remaining two being held by independents.[21]

Fraser's later acknowledgement that, just as had occurred in 1974, his party could not have denied Supply once the half-Senate election had been granted by the Governor-General, simply highlights the fact that Kerr's action in dismissing Whitlam had little to do with an ongoing parliamentary crisis or the absence of Supply, but was a political decision taken in order to avoid a particular outcome—the half-Senate election itself. In appointing Fraser Prime Minister—who was also at that point without Supply—Kerr was quite prepared to allow Fraser as the appointed Prime Minister to go back and test the Senate on Supply, but he was not prepared to allow Whitlam, armed with the half-Senate election, to do the same. At the very least, Kerr should have granted Whitlam the half-Senate election conditional on the passage of Supply for the duration of the election, just as Hasluck had done the previous year.

An explosive revelation from a long-embargoed interview with Fraser further challenges our fundamental understanding of the dismissal of the Whitlam government in relation to this question of Supply. It now appears that the very basis of Whitlam's dismissal, and Fraser's appointment, as Prime Minister—the need to secure Supply—was a constitutional and political charade. In this previously unpublished interview Fraser makes the extraordinary claim that the provision of Supply was *not* in fact a condition of his appointment as Prime Minister at all.

Fraser makes this devastating admission in his interview conducted in 1987 with former Labor Minister Clyde Cameron for the National Library of Australia. At Fraser's request the interview was then embargoed until 2012 and it has only recently been made available. Asked specifically whether the provision of Supply was a condition of his appointment as Prime Minister, Fraser replied without any hesitation, 'No, it wasn't'. In a further dramatic historical unravelling Fraser then revealed that, even had he not secured Supply through the Senate on the afternoon of 11 November 1975, Kerr would not have dismissed him as Prime Minister and that he would have gone to the 1975 election as Prime Minister, without Supply.

A shocked Clyde Cameron drew out the implications of this startling exchange in his immediate response to Fraser: 'You would have gone to an election without Supply, and you would have been in breach of one of the conditions that Kerr had laid down.' Fraser did not disagree with this, suggesting that the Coalition might even have won a few more seats had he done so. Either way, he told Cameron, it would have been the Labor party's fault had he been unable to gain Supply because that could only have happened if the Labor party had 'changed its mind about Supply in the Senate'.

Despite Kerr's insistence that securing Supply was at the heart of the dismissal, Fraser maintained that his own failure to secure Supply would not have led to his dismissal and that Kerr would not have dismissed him for a denial of Supply as he had dismissed Whitlam: 'I don't *think* the Governor-General would have had much other course ... I think it would have been a little difficult sacking a second (laughing) Prime Minister and re-appointing the first one sacked'.[22]

It has taken forty years for Fraser's intention to continue as Prime Minister should he have failed to secure Supply on 11 November 1975 to be uncovered, and it finally answers one of the perennial puzzles in the dynamics of the dismissal: how could Malcolm Fraser have guaranteed the Governor-General that he could secure Supply through the Senate when he, like Whitlam, could not guarantee the numbers? The answer now is clear; he didn't. In his own words Fraser merely 'believed we could get Supply through', not that he would get it through. That Kerr refused to allow Whitlam the opportunity to return to the Senate with the half-Senate election pending the passage of Supply—the opportunity he was prepared to give Fraser—reinforces the view that Supply was only ever a constructed catalyst for dismissal. The purported need to secure Supply in order to secure government was nothing more than a means to an end, and not an end in itself.

In unusually strident editorials the day after the dismissal, in which the Governor-General was accused of 'violating the spirit of representative democracy', the Melbourne *Age* and the *Sydney Morning Herald* were among the few newspapers to recognise Hasluck's resolution of the 1974 threat to block Supply as the model for what Kerr ought to have done. Both these major dailies argued that Kerr should have accepted Whitlam's proper advice to call the half-Senate election, conditional on the provision of Supply, rather than taking the drastic step of dismissal, which the *Sydney Morning Herald* described as a 'rush to judgment' and a 'Yarralumla *coup d'état'*:

Equally, we should like to know if Sir John considered the possibility of urging Mr. Fraser to allow the Senate to pass interim Supply so that a half-Senate election could be held. If Mr. Fraser had refused, Sir John might then have given more consideration to the proposition that a half-Senate election could be held even without Supply being passed ... At least a delayed decision would have enabled him to have further talks with Mr. Whitlam. After all, the Constitution does require the Governor-General to listen to the advice of the Prime Minister of the day. On the evidence of his statement yesterday, Sir John seems to have been more impressed by the advice of the

Chief Justice, Sir Garfield Barwick.[23]

The absence of the decision to call the half-Senate election from many of the popular accounts of the dismissal has fed into the portrayal of Whitlam as guileless, lacking strategic imperative and impervious to any resolution of the crisis in the Senate. The facts simply tell us otherwise.

Kerr's 'Statement of Reasons', with its incomplete chronology and depiction of the half-Senate election as a possibility, not a fact, was a damaging distortion of the events of the previous five days, which helped cast the historical record for years to come. In it and in subsequent works on the dismissal, Whitlam's decision to call the half-Senate election was largely seen as itself an afterthought, taken in haste and under pressure on the morning of 11 November as he sought a solution to a crisis that had already overtaken him.

With the compelling drama of the dismissal itself still unfolding like a political reality show—as parliament resumed, the crowds on the steps of parliament house surged, the Governor-General's official secretary prorogued parliament and Whitlam delivered the impassioned, unforgettable and impromptu 'Well may we say' speech, the fact of the half-Senate election was quickly forgotten. The narrative trajectory of the dismissal finds its natural endpoint with Whitlam and Kerr in the Governor-General's study at Yarralumla, at the point of the dismissal itself. What came after, and before, was easily eclipsed by the spectacle of the dismissal.

In this truncated version of events, the afternoon session of parliament, as both the Senate and the House of Representatives resumed after lunch, receded from view just as quickly as the half-Senate election. It was then, in the shadow of the dismissal late on the afternoon of 11 November 1975, that the Governor-General made his final conclusive move against Whitlam. It was a move that was more shocking, more constitutionally insolent and more imperious even than the dismissal of the Prime Minister four hours earlier. This was Sir John Kerr's second dismissal, the dismissal of the parliament itself.

5

SIR JOHN KERR'S SECOND DISMISSAL

MUCH OF THE history presents the hour before parliament resumed at 2pm on 11 November 1975 with this striking image at its heart: Whitlam, thinking more about his stomach than his tactics, headed for the Lodge and a hefty steak for lunch, drawing his key advisers and senior members of the House of Representatives around him—and forgot to tell the Senate! It's a story so often told that it now appears beyond dispute, as one of the few apparently uncontested elements in the history of the dismissal. Referring to Whitlam's 'misguided response to the dismissal', it has been suggested, for instance, that Whitlam could have obstructed Kerr's actions if only he had told the Senate: 'If Whitlam had immediately turned his attention to denying Fraser Supply, then Kerr's strategy could have been at risk'.[1] In this view Whitlam is self-absorbed, bereft of strategy, wilfully ignorant of the significance of the Senate, and a player in his own demise.

It is a fundamentally flawed analysis, written with the conviction of hindsight. Although we now know that Kerr had set Fraser the apparently critical condition of ensuring Supply—how on earth was Whitlam to know that? After all, Whitlam did not even know that Fraser was already Prime Minister, let alone the conditions on which he had been appointed. How was Whitlam to know that as he left Yarralumla, using the Prime Minister's entrance for the last time, a door was opening at the other end of the corridor as the Leader of the Opposition, Fraser, emerged with the Governor-General's official secretary, David Smith? How was Whitlam to know that at the very time he was being dismissed in the Governor-General's study, Fraser was already at Yarralumla, ensconced with Smith and waiting to be appointed himself?

The deception visited on Whitlam by the Governor-General and the Leader of the Opposition before the dismissal continued unabated. Everything that followed in both Houses of parliament that afternoon needs to be seen in light of this irredeemable disadvantage of deception and ignorance that Whitlam faced as he searched for a political solution with both hands tied behind his back, and his feet not far behind. The idea of thwarting the very thing he had been urging for the last four weeks—the passage of Supply—simply never entered his head. Why would he try to block Supply when he had no idea that Fraser was already Prime Minister and moreover he believed that he would be back in government by the end of the day?

Whitlam's unshakeable conviction that the political institutions would function as they should is matched only by his ignorance of what had already been done and would continue to be done to usurp the role of parliament in the formation of government. He rang Margaret again to tell her, now more confidently, that he would be back in government as soon as the House of Representatives had reconvened. The motion for the House drawn up by Whitlam while at the Lodge with his advisers and colleagues shows him to be unaware of Fraser's immediate ascension: 'That this House declares that it has confidence in the Whitlam Government and that this House informs Her Majesty the Queen that if His Excellency purports to commission the honourable member for Wannon as Prime Minister the House does not have confidence in him or any government he forms'.[2]

As Whitlam entered the House of Representatives for the start of the afternoon session at 2pm, his strategy was as clear as it was simple: the Labor Senators would continue with their efforts to force a vote to pass Supply, and Whitlam would obtain a renewed motion of confidence from the House of Representatives and again form government.

This was a critical moment in our history. The fate of two governments—Whitlam's and Fraser's—depended on the outcome of events in the House of Representatives that afternoon and yet this short post-dismissal sitting has been so readily forgotten to history. It is an unfortunate occlusion, not only for the history of the dismissal but also for our political history in general. For the parliamentary session of the afternoon of 11 November 1975 is surely the most absorbing, compelling politics in action that we have ever witnessed. It is also a rare instance in which the political theatre of the parliament mirrors the momentous import of its resolutions.

Why have the actions taken in the House following the dismissal of the Whitlam government been overlooked in the popular history? By the time of the dismissal the Senate had been the focus of parliamentary crisis and divisive debate for four weeks. It was there that the Opposition Senators had refused to allow a vote on the government's Supply bills and where the bills had been stalled since 16 October. The month-long parliamentary stand-off had come to be seen as a contest between the House of Representatives and the Senate, in which the Senate—as the chamber in control of the budget bills—held all the cards. And so, even after Whitlam's dismissal, the actions in the Senate continued to be the focus of attention—more out of habit than appropriate analysis. Proceedings in the House on the afternoon of 11 November 1975, by contrast, had been almost totally overlooked.

Lost in this continued focus on events in the Senate and the question of Supply was any recognition of Whitlam's post-dismissal strategy, which was based entirely on the actions of the House of Representatives. The continued focus on the Senate also eschewed the fundamental role of the House of Representatives in those vital hours after the dismissal. Throughout the weeks of the crisis Whitlam had repeatedly referred to the House of Representatives as 'the people's House', emphasising both its democratic mandate and its definitive role in the formation of government, as the House in which governments are made and unmade. It should hardly be surprising then that it was to the House of Representatives that Whitlam turned, having just experienced what he described as the greatest shock of his life, as he sought to find the way to return to office.

Confusion, chaos, distress, disbelief, triumphalism—for two hours the House of Representatives on the afternoon of 11 November 1975 had it all. The public gallery seethed as the last seats filled, politicians on the floor were in disarray and many were still unaware the government had been dismissed, and Whitlam himself was unaware that Fraser was already Prime Minister. Fraser delivered his first statement for the afternoon at 2.34pm: 'The Governor-General has commissioned me this afternoon to form a Government'.[3] This was the first that Whitlam knew of Fraser's appointment as Prime Minister and in the ensuing uproar Hansard reporters struggled to keep up.

At 3pm, Whitlam finally rose to speak, and with the House in turmoil he moved a simple motion of no confidence, or 'want of confidence', in Fraser as Prime Minister, advising the Governor-General to call on Whitlam as the leader with the confidence of the House of Representatives, to again form government: 'That this House expresses its want of confidence in the Prime

Minister [Fraser] and requests Mr Speaker forthwith to advise His Excellency the Governor-General to call on the honourable member for Werriwa [Whitlam] to form a government'.[4]

The no-confidence motion against Fraser as Prime Minister and advising the Governor-General to restore the Whitlam government to office was carried by ten votes. The Speaker was then sent to present the motion to the Governor-General, to inform him that the House of Representatives did not have confidence in the Fraser government and calling on him to commission a new government led by Whitlam.

At this moment, Kerr's action in dismissing Whitlam had completely derailed. No government had ever continued in office following the passage of a motion of no confidence against it. The Governor-General would have no choice but to reinstate Whitlam as Prime Minister as the leader with the confidence of the House of Representatives, and now with his budget also passed, since the Senate had at 2.24pm passed the Supply bills that had been stalled for the preceding month. Whitlam fully believed that at this point he would be recommissioned as Prime Minister and that his government would be restored to office—this was Whitlam's strategy, and it should have been the outcome.

On hearing that Fraser had been appointed Prime Minister, Billy McMahon's private secretary Robert Ashley expostulated on the inevitable futility of the Governor-General's actions—Whitlam would only be restored to office as soon as the House reconvened and passed a motion of no confidence in Fraser. 'No-one can continue in office after that', Ashley told McMahon. McMahon disagreed: 'Malcolm Fraser is the only man in Australia who would', he replied.[5] McMahon was right. He was, and he did. Fraser has the ignominy of being the only Prime Minister in Australia's history to have continued in office following the receipt of a motion of no confidence against him.

Whitlam reserved his strongest possible criticism of Malcolm Fraser for this, his decision to ignore the motion of no confidence of the House of Representatives and to remain in office regardless, for his failure to protect the House of Representatives and the processes of democratic government. Whitlam thundered to a campaign meeting the week after the dismissal: 'He should have returned to Government House at once, tendered his resignation to the Governor-General and advised him to call the leader of the party that commanded the support of the Parliament. This is the course that honour and precedent and history have sanctioned'.[6]

The single most important resolution the House of Representatives can ever make, the resolution by which governments are made and unmade, is a motion of confidence in the House of Representatives. It is the defining feature of the Westminster system and the *sine qua non* of democratic government. The continuation of Fraser in office, despite the no-confidence motion against him, profoundly challenged the very essence of parliamentary democracy and its established political processes. The repudiation of this foundational role of the House of Representatives in the formation of government was nothing less than a repudiation of parliamentary democracy itself.

This was Kerr's second dismissal, the dismissal of the parliament itself. In the forty-five minutes since Fraser's announcement to the Parliament that the Governor-General had appointed him Prime Minister, he had lost five motions in the House of Representatives, including a motion of no confidence by ten votes. This politically defining sequence of events in the House of Representatives following the dismissal has been too readily overlooked, seen as just another quirk in the tumultuous events of a singularly tumultuous day. In an extraordinary omission, Fraser's co-authored memoirs make no mention at all of the motion of no confidence against him.[7]

It was only with the long-overdue statement from former Justice Sir Anthony Mason that we now know that once again he played a critical role in the actions of the Governor-General in the final throes of the dismissal. Soon after the motion of no confidence in Fraser had passed and, with the Speaker soon to see him, the Governor-General telephoned Mason. Essentially Kerr asked him: What should I do? I have appointed a Prime Minister, Malcolm Fraser, who does not have the confidence of the House of Representatives, the House of Representatives has expressed its confidence in Gough Whitlam and has advised me to recommission the Whitlam government.

With the passage of Supply through the Senate there was also now no barrier to Whitlam re-forming government, although there is no suggestion from Mason that Kerr even raised the fact of the successful passage of Supply with him, or that he saw it as relevant to his apparent quandary. In his public statement, released after thirty-seven years of silence, Mason gives this remarkable episode scant consideration. There are just two sentences on his discussion with the Governor-General at this defining moment, the outcome of which would seal the respective fates of the Whitlam and the Fraser governments.

Mason's response to Kerr was elegant in its simplicity and devastating in its implications: the motion of no confidence in Fraser, he told Kerr, was 'irrelevant'. It was a stark repudiation of the defining element of the Westminster system, that governments are made and unmade on the floor of the House of Representatives, the ultimate expression of the decision of the electorate. It is simply astounding that a sitting Justice of the High Court could consider a motion of no confidence in the Prime Minister by the House of Representatives *irrelevant.*

In reality, there was no quandary for the Governor-General in any of this. The institutions of government had performed exactly as Whitlam had believed they would and on which belief he had structured his post-dismissal strategy. Just as he had said from the outset, the deferral of Supply in the Senate had been a political matter and it would be resolved politically. Whitlam had resolved it first through his decision to call a half-Senate election and he had resolved it a second time through securing the confidence of the House of Representatives. It was the Governor-General who had denied him each time. Kerr would now also deny the parliament, refusing to see the Speaker of the House of Representatives, or even to receive the motion of no confidence against his appointed Prime Minister, Fraser. Instead, Kerr moved immediately to close down the parliament with Fraser still in office, keeping the Speaker waiting for over an hour until 4.45pm. The House of Representatives, scheduled to reconvene at 5.30pm, would not meet again.

It was, as political journalist Mungo MacCallum described it, 'a reassertion of the divine right of kings'.[8]

6

'A VERY BRITISH COUP'

'Any intervention by us (in effect in Australian domestic politics) could have serious implications and both the nature and the timing thereof would need very careful consideration.'[1]

IN THE AFTERMATH of Sir John Kerr's dismissal of the Whitlam government, persistent speculation lingered over the possible role of the Crown. The Governor-General was, after all, the Queen's representative in Australia and his extraordinary action had been taken in her name, yet on the basis of unspecified 'reserve powers' long since thought extinct.[2] The disclaimers began at once. Any involvement of the Queen or the British government was immediately and emphatically denied, most clearly and conclusively by the Queen's private secretary, Sir Martin Charteris, in a letter to the former Speaker of the House of Representatives, Gordon Scholes:

the Australian Constitution firmly places the prerogative powers of the Crown in the hands of the Governor-General as the representative of The Queen of Australia. The only person competent to commission an Australian Prime Minister is the Governor-General, and The Queen has no part in the decisions which the Governor-General must take in accordance with the Constitution ... it would not be proper for her to intervene in person in matters which are so clearly placed within the jurisdiction of the Governor-General.[3]

Charteris' letter reflected the official 'line to be taken' that had been worked up by the powerful Foreign and Commonwealth Office (FCO) at Whitehall during the weeks in which Supply had been blocked in the Senate.[4] It presented a simple, straightforward and seemingly incontrovertible denial of British involvement in the

Governor-General's unprecedented action in dismissing without warning a government that retained the confidence of the House of Representatives. In the months to come, the essence of Charteris' defining statement would be quoted repeatedly by British officials, a reassurance of arms-length imperial propriety and vice-regal independence, when responding to every inquiry, concern or outrage that followed the dismissal.

It was a carefully constructed sophistry in which every word had been chosen with singular purpose—to mask the truth of British involvement in the dismissal of the Whitlam government.

Clues to the subterfuge can be seen in its precision; Charteris' insistent denial was cast in the narrowest terms as relating to the Governor-General's power to commission the Australian Prime Minister, to 'matters ... within the jurisdiction of the Governor-General' and, most importantly, in its specific reference to 'Her Majesty as Queen of Australia' playing no part in the Governor-General's decisions. Charteris neither refers to nor denies the second and less widely-known avenue for Royal involvement in domestic Australian political matters, through Her Majesty the Queen as the Queen of the United Kingdom. And that Queen's connection was not to the Australian Prime Minister but to the Australian states, four of which were led by conservative Premiers fiercely opposed to the Whitlam government.

For there were two Queens in this hybrid Australian constitutional monarchy and it was what was done by and in the name of the Queen of the United Kingdom that would be pivotal in the dismissal of the Whitlam government.

It began on 15 October 1975 with telegram no.869 to the FCO from the British High Commission in Canberra on the 'Australian Political Situation':

> Mr Fraser has announced that federal Opposition in Senate will block Supply until Mr Whitlam agrees to federal elections. Mr Whitlam has indicated that he will not request dissolution of House of Representatives but will seek to hold half-Senate elections due before first of July 1976.[5]

At first glance this was a routine notification by the British High Commission of the latest breach of parliamentary convention by the Opposition in refusing to allow a vote in the Senate on the Supply bills, and of Whitlam's intention to call the half-Senate election. But the archival records of the FCO and the High Commission paint a very different picture. This apparently unremarkable telegram triggered an exceptional degree of consternation beyond its immediate significance, sparking a series of internal deliberations and conjectures. Their disquiet was not, as might have been expected, over the Opposition's unprecedented obstruction in blocking the government's Supply bills in the Senate—on this there is no adverse comment—but over the half-Senate election itself. That this was the focus of British concern is all the more surprising given that not only was the half-Senate election due, it was also a constitutional requirement that Whitlam call it within one year from 1 July 1975.[6]

Yet despite its constitutional inevitability the FCO and the High Commission regarded the half-Senate election as the critical issue in the political drama unfolding in Canberra, as a 'contingency' to prepare for and ultimately to avoid, rather than a regular part of the Australian electoral cycle to be protected and respected. Most disturbingly, by late October the FCO had proceeded to a lengthy consideration of 'the question of our possible involvement in the half-Senate election'.[7]

It is impossible to overstate the significance of these words—'the question of our possible involvement in the half-Senate election'—for with them the FCO had entered into precisely the area that Charteris would later deny, of British involvement in Australian domestic politics.

Files of the FCO held in the UK National Archives show that this involvement came not with the act of dismissal itself but with decisions made and actions taken in the weeks before it, which led Sir John Kerr to understand his primary duty as

Governor-General as being 'to protect' the Queen—even at the cost of Australian democratic practice.[8] As the half-Senate election loomed more firmly on the horizon, the 'problem' of the pending half-Senate election would become a crisis, and 'one we would wish if at all possible to avoid'.[9]

The question was, why? Why would the British mandarins at Whitehall show such extreme concern over a routine part of the Australian democratic process, a regular half-Senate election, sufficient to drive it to intervene in order to avoid that election *if at all possible*? The answer lies in the heavily redacted files of the FCO in the UK National Archives, and in the files of the Royal family and Sir Martin Charteris in the Royal Archives, which are closed to public view. While much remains hidden, in particular the secret 'Palace letters' between Kerr and the Queen in the months before the dismissal, it is time this story of imperial presumption and intrigue was told.

In the Australian–British relationship there was no bigger player than the

Foreign and Commonwealth Office. The FCO had grown out of the old Colonial Office and retained much of its organisational culture.[10] It had not exactly been difficult for the FCO to maintain the quasi-imperial mind-set implicit in its provenance, and it had grown comfortable with the certainties of the post-war Menzies coalition governments. Liberal Prime Minister, Sir Robert Menzies, an avowed monarchist and noted Anglophile, personified that dominion subservience with his unctuous declaration of Royal devotion during the Queen's 1963 visit to Australia: 'I did but see her passing by and yet I love her 'til I die.'[11]

The election of the Whitlam government shook the FCO out of its unchallenged complacency. Just as the conservative parties in Australia, experiencing unwelcome opposition for the first time in 23 years, strained at the reality of the opposition benches and shadow ministries they had never known before, so too the FCO could not and would not adjust to the policies and expectations of a new government intent on establishing a more independent relationship with the former imperial power. Unwilling to accommodate these new parameters, the FCO's longstanding networks, collegial connections and personal friendships, their implicit understandings of how things should be done continued unchecked despite the change of government.

In June 1973, the British conservative Prime Minister, Edward Heath, met the Australian leader of the Opposition, Billy Snedden, in London. Their meeting was no secret and was known to Whitlam's office, the content of their conversation however, most definitely was not.[12] The meeting was brief, 45 minutes at number 10 Downing Street, and focused on the constitutional issues Whitlam was pursuing with the British government, to which the Opposition and the conservative states were furiously opposed. As the meeting ended, Snedden asked Heath for a letter setting out the key points of their conversation. Heath's office was horrified and flatly refused; 'the Prime Minister would not want his conversation with Mr Snedden or the contents of this letter to be quoted or attributed in any way to him or to the British government'.[13] The FCO was even more alarmed; 'it could be dangerous for the Prime Minister [Heath] to confirm in writing what he has said to Mr Snedden'.[14]

The 'danger' to Heath in merely confirming his discussion with Snedden lay in its manifest impropriety. It was completely indefensible for the British Prime Minister to discuss these constitutional matters with the Australian leader of the Opposition while they were under discussion with the Australian Prime Minister, as the FCO itself acknowledged. Despite this, Heath and his advisors wanted these discussions with Snedden to continue, yet feared the reaction should Whitlam hear of them; 'Mr Whitlam has already expressed objections to the British government discussing these matters ... with Australian state governments, it seems likely that he would object even more strongly if he knew that the [British] Prime Minister had discussed them with the leader of the Australian opposition'. And so, the FCO proposed a solution as reprehensible as it was simple—secrecy from and deception of the Australian Prime Minister.[15] Future contact between Snedden and Heath, the FCO proposed, would be on a direct private secretary to private secretary basis, preferably by telephone rather than in writing, and 'nothing should pass through the Australian High Commission'. By avoiding the Australian High Commission the secret Heath–Snedden communications would also avoid the risk of discovery by Whitlam's new Australian High Commissioner, the Labor stalwart and former Senator, John Armstrong.[16] The key proviso put to Snedden was that his conversations with Heath would remain secret and were never to be attributed to the British Prime Minister.[17]

And so it continued throughout the term of the Whitlam government, in what became a pattern of routine secrecy and undermining. Whitlam faced the bulwark of a British bureaucracy infused with longstanding personal connections, a partisan political outlook, disdain for Whitlam's personal style and a marked indifference to his core policy of ending the 'colonial relics' in the British–Australian relationship. The term 'colonial relics' had really stung British authorities when first used by Whitlam's Attorney-General, Senator Lionel Murphy, at a press conference in London in 1973—a term which the FCO considered 'provocative' and which Whitlam happily adopted as his own.[18] As he bluntly told the new British Labour Prime Minister Harold Wilson the following year, 'all these colonial relics were incompatible with the position of Australia as a separate, sovereign country'.[19]

Billy Snedden's meeting with the British Prime Minister was followed just days later by the former Australian High Commissioner and Liberal party grandee, Sir Alexander Downer, who was granted a rare private meeting with Heath.[20] The determinedly Anglophile Downer had been appointed by the Menzies government, in which he had been Minister for Immigration, and he had been Australian High Commissioner for nearly a decade until his resignation in October 1972.[21] Whitlam's new High Commissioner, John Armstrong, had created a storm before he even left Sydney by announcing that Australia must one day become a republic, and created a further storm on arrival in London with the memorable remark that, 'my office is on the first floor of Australia House, and the door's open. So is the bar'.[22] A man less like Sir Alexander Downer would be difficult to imagine.

Downer had sought an urgent meeting with Heath to discuss the dramatic shift in Australian foreign policy and to warn him of Whitlam's 'anti-British, anti-colonial line'—that Whitlam was 'flirting with the third world', that he had just visited Prime Minister Indira Gandhi in India, and that his deputy Foreign Minister was touring 'black Africa'.[23] Downer and Heath met at Downing Street, six months after the election of the Whitlam government, as though nothing had changed. Downer was close enough and familiar enough to Heath to presume to tell him straight up how the British government ought to respond to Whitlam's efforts to end the residual colonial ties—tell Whitlam that the British government could do nothing unless all the states agreed. Which is exactly what Heath did.

In January 1975, the FCO itself entertained two of the conservative state Premiers most stridently opposed to Whitlam's independent 'new nationalism', Queensland's Joh Bjelke-Petersen and Western Australia's Sir Charles Court. The Premiers were welcomed by the FCO in their departmental offices on a formal visit during which they were entertained by the Conservative Party central office and the London branch of the Liberal Party of Australia. Despite the FCO's earlier insistence to Whitlam that it did not engage in 'substantive discussions with the states', during this meeting with the conservative Premiers it did just that.[24] The FCO's involvement with such a partisan retinue earned a strong rebuke from British Labour MP, Russell Kerr, who complained that by meeting the Premiers at the height of Whitlam's grave difficulties with the states, the FCO risked becoming involved 'in a very considerable struggle in Australia between the Labour (sic) Government and the Right-wing group of "states-rights" Premiers'.[25] Elevating the status of the conservative Premiers only encouraged Bjelke-Petersen's troublesome delusions of state grandeur—the Queensland Premier had recently tried to negotiate a trade agreement with Japan and was seeking to declare the Queen the 'Queen of Queensland' in a failed effort to entrench the monarchy in his state against what he saw as Whitlam's incipient republicanism.

The FCO's connections with conservative state Premiers and opposition politicians, and its facilitation of secret communications between Heath and Snedden, were both improper and deeply partisan as the schism in Australian politics intensified. This continuing connection with those now on the opposition benches reflected the yearning for another time that permeates these files, for a return to the settled politics and comfortable certainties of the Menzies era, in which everything and everyone was in its place. The damage done to a post-colonial relationship which rested on mutual trust, respect and transparency, could not have been more profound.

The single most important means through which the FCO conducted and justified its elevated connections with the states and its prevarications over Whitlam's agenda of independent nationalism, was through the obscure notion of the bifurcated Queen. In this distinction, there were two Queens dealing with Australian matters—the Queen of Australia who dealt with the Commonwealth and the Queen of the UK who dealt with the states. For all but the most ardent legal scholar this technical division of Royal form and function was virtually unknown, a constitutional nicety which had had no bearing on the practical reality of British–Australian relations for decades.[26]

This untroubled duality changed with the election of the Whitlam government and the FCO breathed new life into the anachronism of the two Queens. Animated by a determination to frustrate Whitlam's efforts to end the 'colonial relics', the FCO bolstered its relationship with the Australian states, treating them as political and constitutional equivalents of the Commonwealth and according them remarkable access and status. The duality of the Royal persona, itself a colonial relic, would become a critical factor in the dismissal of the Whitlam government.

It went something like this. The Queen of Australia was advised by the Australian Prime Minister, Gough Whitlam, on matters relating to the Commonwealth, through the Governor-General.[27] The Queen of the UK by contrast was advised on Australian state matters by British ministers, with input from the Australian state Premiers through their Governors. The critical difference between them was this: the Queen of Australia dealt with the Prime Minister of Australia, whereas the Queen of the UK dealt with the British ministers, the FCO and the state Premiers—without any input from, and potentially secret from, the Australian Prime Minister.

The legal principle of the two Queens reflected the different post-colonial status of the

Commonwealth and the states. The Commonwealth was independent in its sphere and directly advised the Queen, whereas the states remained, in the eyes of the FCO, 'in a quasi-colonial relationship with the United Kingdom'—they had not yet even reached the stage of 'colonial relics'.[28] In this unique relationship between the states and the Crown, it was the British ministers who advised the Queen of the UK in relation to Australian state matters, and that advice would be based on the interests of the UK independent of, and at times even contrary to, the advice of the states.

Particularly significant in this line of communication between the states and the Queen of the UK, was the powerful central role played by the FCO. The FCO was the initial point of contact for the state Governors in their communication with the Queen of the UK, and it was the FCO that advised the British ministers on the advice they would then give to the Queen. In these 'quasi-colonial' matters, the FCO's advice to ministers was rarely, if ever, disputed. Critically for the Whitlam government, then in the midst of its titanic political struggle with the Opposition federally and the four non-Labor states, this line of communication with the reinvigorated Queen of the UK enabled the states and the FCO and the Palace to communicate, potentially without informing the Australian Prime Minister. The abstruse legal principle of the bifurcated Queen had been transformed into a powerful political weapon—secrecy.

The files show how this was done. A letter from the British High Commission in Canberra early in 1975 headed 'Telling the Feds and the States', provides rare evidence of secrecy from Whitlam as a direct instruction from the FCO, and of the consternation this caused among High Commission staff. It relates to the meetings and communications with the conservative state Premiers and refers to a recent 'instruction' from the FCO that the High Commission not inform the Whitlam government of its communications with the Western Australian Liberal Premier Court.

The instruction to keep Court's communication secret from Whitlam was clearly irregular and alarmed the usually unquestioning staff of the High Commission, who disputed that such secrecy was 'normal practice' as the FCO claimed and requested 'supporting evidence of past practice' of it:

> In FCO telegram no.917 of 23 December 1974 we were instructed on the basis of 'normal practice' not to inform the Australian government of a communication from Sir Charles Court about his visit to London. None of us here, even those with long memories and experience of dealing with the plethora of governments in Australia, could put his finger on chapter and verse to such a precedent.[29]

A margin note from the FCO adds to the narrative of back-room intrigue laced with quasi-imperial *hauteur* and tells us a great deal about what was driving their disdain—Whitlam's determination to end the 'colonial relics'. This dismissive note, redolent with the weary exasperation typical of much of the bureaucratic commentary dealing with Whitlam and in obvious mimicry of him, reads, 'We play this on an *ad hoc basis.* If we have good reason to want to tell the federal government of the state communication we will do so, that is our privilege as the "colonial power"'. From this position of imperial 'privilege', the FCO would decide what the Australian Prime Minister could know of their communications with the states and when he could know it.

With such a closed channel of communication with the states, one that kept Whitlam locked out on a 'need to know' basis, the power to determine what was to be considered a state matter, and therefore to be dealt with by the Queen of the UK on the advice of her British ministers and not by the Queen of Australia on Whitlam's advice, held particular significance. During the Whitlam government, the FCO saw almost all constitutional matters as necessarily also state matters—an easy step in a federation as there are few national matters which would not also impinge on one or more of the states. The states became the means of thwarting the government's agenda for ending the remaining constitutional ties with the UK, with the FCO raising insurmountable problems over possible state issues at every point.

Whitlam had from the outset pressed the British government for all communications with the states to be made through the Governor-General and not the state Governors, in an effort to cut across the residual 'dominion' status with the states and their line of communication with the British government, the FCO and the Palace, which he well understood could cause problems for his government.[30] His concerns were not misplaced. The proposal was given short-shrift and the FCO refused to be drawn on any of Whitlam's efforts to end the residual colonial constitutional entanglements that did not also include the support of all six states—an impossible barrier to change.[31]

This can be seen most clearly in relation to the residual right of appeal from some state courts to the Privy Council, which Whitlam found abhorrent and was absolutely determined to end; 'We are a separate country from Britain.

We are an entirely independent country'
he told reporters in 1973 after his first
visit to the UK as Prime Minister, clearly
frustrated at the lack of progress on
this 'absurd' and 'ludicrous' situation:

> It is absurd that citizens of any
> country can litigate their differences
> before a court sitting in another
> country, composed of Judges
> appointed by the Government of
> that other country ... I am
> embarrassed and also I am
> ashamed [that] the Australian
> States are now asking the British
> Government to keep the Privy
> Council to save them from
> Australia's own courts.[32]

The following year an exasperated
Whitlam asked the new British Labour
Prime Minister, Harold Wilson, how he
would feel in such a situation and
whether 'the British government would
allow a dispute between two British
citizens to go to the Court of another
country'.[33] The problematised
response to the Whitlam government's
moves to end residual Privy Council
appeals could not have been more
different from the smooth and

unchallenged decision by the Holt Liberal/Country party government six years earlier to limit appeals from the High Court to the Privy Council. Holt described it as 'an expression of national maturity', which was also Labor policy.[34] The Holt government's decision elicited little concern over potential state Constitutional issues and was welcomed by the British Prime Minister without question.[35]

In all these glimpses into the inner dealings of Whitehall one thing is clear—that the FCO interpreted these relationships, communication channels, 'past practices' and post-colonial imperatives, with utter inconsistency. Established processes were claimed and acted on with great insistence, only later to be refuted and acted against with equal insistence. They became a means of controlling communications between Whitlam and the Palace by constructing a myth of Royal immutability—that just as things had always been done, so they must always be done.

Two of the most strongly asserted immutabilities of the relationship between Australia and the Crown were the inter-related imperatives that the Queen must never be faced with conflicting advice and that she must always remain neutral in matters of domestic politics. For the Queen to receive conflicting advice would require her to act as a person and not an institution, to exercise individual agency and to make a choice, ceasing to be neutral. It was this exercise of personal choice, the FCO claimed, that would definitively involve the Queen in domestic political matters and 'draw her into controversy', and this would never do.[36] Sir Martin Charteris insisted, 'We must not allow a situation to arise in which The Queen can receive contrary advice from two different Ministers'.[37] Although Whitlam pointed out that the obvious solution to any apparent problem of the Queen receiving conflicting advice from her British and Australian ministers was that the British government should simply give the Queen the same advice as the Australian government, the fear of 'conflicting advice' became another means of constraining Whitlam's advice.[38]

Neither of these allied claims of an absolute prohibition on the Queen receiving conflicting advice and her essential neutrality, was in fact the case. The Queen did receive potentially conflicting advice, as she acknowledged in her speech opening the Australian Parliament in 1974, revealing that she had acted on the advice of both her British and Australian ministers in relation to a Privy Council matter.[39] There had been several other occasions on which the Queen did what was required in the face of 'conflicting considerations' and simply reached a decision with her advisors, in particular in relation to Australian state matters.[40] And despite Charteris' insistence to the contrary, the Queen also held strong personal opinions on policy issues and she was not afraid to express them. She had engaged in robust policy discussions with Gough Whitlam during their private meetings and had even sought to change his position on some of the constitutional matters he was trying to progress through the unresponsive British bureaucracy.[41] For example, the Queen succeeded in convincing Whitlam to drop his plans that she no longer sign and receive diplomatic Letters of Credence.[42]

Throughout this time the Queen's private secretary, Sir Martin Charteris, maintained a regular line of communication with the FCO about Whitlam's efforts to end the colonial ties, including reporting on Whitlam's highly confidential private meetings with the Queen.[43] With Charteris as the lynchpin between the FCO and the Palace regarding the states, he was able to serve as an informal channel of information about Whitlam's 'confidential' conversations with the Palace, and to receive 'advice with a small "a"' in return.[44] The Queen's meetings with her Commonwealth Prime Ministers were understood to be held in the strictest confidence, a principle which Charteris claimed 'has always been observed', and yet which he himself shamelessly breached.[45] In 1973, with the Whitlam government just months old, Charteris provided the FCO with a full account of Whitlam's discussions with the Queen, information which went from there to the British Prime Minister's Department and on to Canadian authorities.[46] This was no inadvertent breach of confidentiality and Charteris was fully aware of the profound failure of trust and governance it constituted, warning the FCO with the greatest of ironies, to 'treat this letter with great confidence'.[47]

Charteris is a spectral presence throughout the FCO files. Although few of his letters remain, he is everywhere among them—letters are circulated to him, memos are written in response to his requests for information, and responses are constructed in deference to him. As the Queen's private secretary, Charteris' correspondence is also Her Majesty's correspondence and it has been placed in the vast and impenetrable Royal archives, safely away from the prying eyes of the Australian public whose history it recounts. A tantalising example occasionally slips through—'folio 141: Sir Martin Charteris' comments about state Ministers having direct access to HM [Her Majesty]'—only to be removed at a later date, replaced by a single sheet of paper with one sentence: 'Document temporarily retained in the Department of origin', and a glimpse of the intrigue still hidden from view.[48]

Where the dual Royal persona and her two channels of communication intersected with the events leading inexorably towards the dismissal, was with the half-Senate election, specifically with the requirement that state Governors issue the necessary writs for the election in their states to take place.

For every one of the 24 previous half-Senate elections, the issuing of writs had been a mere formality and implemented by the states as a matter of course. However, these were not ordinary times and there were few, if any, elements in the parliamentary and electoral process that would not be overturned by the Opposition in its quest to return to office. The minutiae of the issuing of writs through the states provided just one more opportunity for disruption. On 12 October 1975, the Liberal party federal council took the unprecedented step of calling on the four conservative state Premiers to put the interests of the Liberal party ahead of the interests of the electoral process and refuse to issue writs for the half-Senate election.[49] The Liberal party's federal council had reached this reckless decision to subvert the half-Senate election several months earlier. It was a strategy of electoral disruption for base political purposes, protecting the Opposition's numbers in the Senate, which had nothing to do with the blocking of Supply.[50]

The leader of the Opposition, Malcolm Fraser, dismissed the half-Senate election as a 'device', a means of avoiding 'the judgment of the people', yet despite Fraser's bravado, the showdown with the conservative states over the issuing of writs was little more than an empty threat.[51] With remarkable prescience Section 11 of the Constitution, 'Failure to choose Senators', deals with precisely this scenario, anticipating just such electoral disregard by a state and enabling the Senate to be constituted even if some states fail to provide representation.[52]

The effect of Section 11 was to neutralise the Opposition's 'threat'. Whitlam dismissed it as 'bluff'.

There was a particular imperative for the non-Labor states to issue writs for the 1975 half-Senate election, given the uniquely placed Senate make-up following the High Court's decision in early October to uphold the Whitlam government's *Senate (Representation of Territories) Act,* delivering for the first time two Senators each for the Northern Territory and the ACT. With those four new Senators together with the two replacement Labor Senators to take their places immediately, a failure to issue the writs would have been a perilous path for the Opposition as it would simply have deprived the coalition in those states of seats in the new Senate. Whitlam had already been advised that the Senate election could take place with the remaining states and the two newly Senate enfranchised Territories.[53]

Whitlam was more appalled at the breach of convention this threat reflected than concerned by it. It would after all be entirely in his government's favour were the conservative states to fail to issue writs as this would only have improved the ALP numbers in the Senate. Whitlam's position on this was clear—should the Liberal party make good its 'threat' to further obstruct the parliamentary process by telling its state Premiers not to issue the writs for their states, then the half-Senate election would take place without them.[54] Faced with the prospect of the half-Senate election going ahead, Whitlam believed the conservative states would fall into line. This was the Opposition's greatest fear, that on calling the half-Senate election, Gough Whitlam held all the cards.

The FCO was, as ever, extremely well informed by its network of coalition 'informants' on the political ramifications of the pending half-Senate election.[55] In early October, with Supply not yet blocked in the Senate, J Hay in the British High Commission in Canberra engineered a discussion with the Opposition assistant whip, Liberal Senator Fred Chaney, ostensibly to discuss constitutional issues and in fact to explore the implications of the half-Senate election for the Opposition.[56] Hay was 'particularly interested in the scenario should Whitlam opt to go for a half-Senate election'. The answer was, dire. On Chaney's estimation, confirmed by polling over the coming weeks, the half-Senate election would result in an improved Senate position for the Labor party at the expense of the coalition and, most importantly, could give it a small majority in the Senate. The half-Senate election would enable the Whitlam government to continue 'relatively unimpeded by the upper House at least until 1 July 1976'.

For the Opposition, this was nothing short of disastrous—their greatest fear was Whitlam's determination to implement the legislated electoral redistributions and end the rural gerrymander that strongly favoured the National/Country Party. The introduction of equalsized electorates would cost the National/Country Party at least five seats and so, the High Commission concluded, 'the opposition ... would be expected to oppose the half-Senate election by all means possible'. Fraser had already discussed the personal implications of this disastrous political outcome with his senior party leaders and it had been agreed that once Whitlam called the half-Senate election the Opposition's high-stakes gamble of constitutional breach and parliamentary disruption would be over. With the half-Senate election in train, Fraser would resign as leader of the Liberal party and Supply would be passed.[57]

There can be no doubt from this and other reports that the FCO well understood the devastating impact of the half-Senate election on the Opposition's political fortunes. These regular reports on 'the Australian political situation' from the British High Commission in Canberra showed the sharply diverging trajectory for the government and opposition in the month before the dismissal.[58] Opinion polls showed a dramatic rise of ALP support during the political stand-off in the Senate, with an increase of 8% in the single week after Supply was blocked.

By 28 October the High Commission reported that the Whitlam government's fortunes had improved a further 7%

over that week, with a staggering 85% of those polled now believing the Whitlam government should be able to serve its three year term; 'Mr Fraser looks to be on the run'.[59] Four days later the High Commission reported that 'Mr Fraser is not onto a winner ... the evidence of the public opinion polls shows that Mr Whitlam's gamble in refusing to be stampeded into seeking a double dissolution might well pay off'.[60] By early November Whitlam's approval rating was leading Fraser's for the first time in months, while 70% of people thought that the Senate should pass Supply.[61]

Most telling was a poll in *The Age* on 5 November for the pending half-Senate election, which showed the Labor party with a commanding lead over the Opposition at 49.2% to 46.7%.[62] On these figures the half-Senate election would give Whitlam what the Opposition most feared, a majority in the Senate at least until the following July. The next day Whitlam told the Governor-General that he intended calling the half-Senate election for 13 December and would announce it in the House of Representatives on 11 November. Their offices exchanged the necessary paperwork and, on the morning of 11 November, Kerr and Whitlam agreed on the wording of the announcement that Whitlam was to make in the House that afternoon. The Opposition's nightmare scenario was now in play.

The Opposition was in a state of 'panic', as veteran journalist Alan Reid described it, over the half-Senate election, acutely aware that the government could return with a majority in the Senate and implement its electoral equity legislation. Most importantly for the trajectory of the half-Senate election is that the FCO was also aware, from no less a source than the Opposition assistant whip, Senator Chaney, that it was precisely because of its immense political significance that the Opposition intended to 'oppose the half-Senate election by all means possible'. Nevertheless, despite its obvious party political implications, the FCO and the High Commission soon joined with the Opposition in railing against 'the half-Senate election issue'.

Within days the FCO's consideration of the question of issuing the writs changed dramatically, intensifying around a new, hypothetical and deeply troubling issue that had not previously been raised in their communications. Overnight the hypothetical situation that some states may refuse to issue writs for the half-Senate election escalated to a 'conflict' between the states and the Commonwealth with alarming and, hypothetical upon hypothetical, repercussions. Referring only to a newspaper report and 'speculation here in Canberra', the BHC and the FCO then envisaged a constitutionally fraught scenario with devastating implications for the Queen(s) and her channels of communication and with the even more fearsome prospect of the Queen receiving 'conflicting advice'.

The narrative of conflict and crisis quickly spiralled into its inevitable if illusory denouement: that, faced with the state Governors refusing to issue the writs, Whitlam would advise Kerr to instruct the Queen to instruct the state Governors to ignore the advice of their own Premiers and instead to issue the writs for the half-Senate election.[63] The Queen(s) then, in this confabulated three-step hypothetical future, would face the prospect of receiving the unthinkable 'conflicting advice', thereby becoming involved in Australian domestic politics. Constitutional law expert Anne Twomey describes the effect of this 'rumour', that 'Mr Whitlam would be advising the Queen of Australia to advise the Queen of the United Kingdom to advise the Governors to issue the writs. The British government was quite aware of this problem and was very concerned about it, and so in the lead-up to the dismissal that was the thing that was spooking the British government.'[64]

The 'problem' that the Queen might receive conflicting advice in relation to the issuing of writs for the half-Senate election soon led to its ineluctable conclusion—that this contingency to follow from the half-Senate election had to be avoided 'if at all possible'. In reaching their ominous conclusion, built on speculation upon speculation, both the FCO and the High Commission reveal an extraordinary ignorance of even the most fundamental aspects of the Australian federal political and constitutional system. In this morass of error and misconception, the half-Senate election was seen purely as a state matter rather than part of the federal electoral cycle; the 1975 half-Senate election which was due at that time was erroneously described as 'early' and therefore as possible grounds for the states to refuse to issue writs; and Whitlam's advice to call it was even seen as of doubtful legality.[65]

Most extreme was the preposterous advice given by the Canadian Senator and expert on Canadian reserve powers, Eugene Forsey, who disputed that there was any such thing as a half-Senate election: 'He could find no mention of such an election in the Australian constitution.'[66] Despite Forsey's breathtaking ignorance of fundamental Australian constitutional reality, Kerr nevertheless considered Forsey to be 'one of the great living authorities on the reserve powers of the Crown' and, in this display of reciprocal approbation, Forsey would later become one of Kerr's keenest constitutional barrackers in support of his dismissal of the Whitlam government.[67]

Here is the archetype of the channel of communication for the Queen of the UK at work. The FCO saw itself as the final arbiter of what to tell the Australian Prime Minister regarding state matters—'that is our right as the "colonial power"'. The FCO reasoned, with trademark ignorance and misunderstanding, that the half-Senate election was purely a state matter because of the requirement for the state Governors to issue writs for their state, which was for them alone to determine—as though the Senate election was akin to a state election rather than a federal one. In this innovative interpretation of both the Australian constitution and political system, the FCO concluded that Senate elections could be deemed to be purely state matters because of the involvement of the state Governors in issuing writs, despite references to Senate elections in the constitution at sections 10 and 11, despite the Territories now also having Senators and despite the fact that they are elections for the federal, not the state, parliament.

These constitutional acrobatics provided the means to involve the Queen of the UK and her British ministers in their contemplations of interference in Australian domestic politics, all of which was unknown to Whitlam. The High Commission set out the role of the Queen of the UK in its justification for possible intervention in Australian domestic politics in order to avoid the feared 'conflicting advice'; 'there are some aspects of the current constitutional deadlock in Australia ... which might conceivably be held to concern British Ministers by virtue of their role in advising the Crown on certain matters concerning the Australian States ... in view of the request by Sir Martin Charteris that the PUS [Permanent Under-Secretary] keep him informed of any situation that might possibly lead to the tendering of conflicting advice to the Queen'.[68]

One of the most remarkable features of this escalating correspondence of secrecy and deception is that nowhere does it canvas what Whitlam actually said he would do should some states refuse to issue the writs. In all this fevered discussion of an imagined looming constitutional crisis over the hypothetical failure to issue writs and over the Queen(s) facing conflicting advice, no-one asked the simple question—what would Whitlam do? Whitlam had already indicated that if the conservative states refused to issue writs, then the half-Senate election would simply go ahead without them. For Whitlam, the hypothetical scenario was simply never an option. Department advice was that, based on the British government's refusal to become involved in the constitutional matters Whitlam had previously raised with them, they would clearly consider this an Australian domestic matter in which they could play no role.[69] Whitlam was, after all, intent on ending the residual colonial ties and was hardly likely to approach the Queen of the UK, a 'foreign monarch' in his words, to deal with the conservative states when the Australian constitution provided for this scenario so clearly.

A report on a meeting between Whitlam and the British High Commissioner, Sir Morrice James, in Canberra on 16 October, the day Supply was first blocked in the Senate, confirms this. Whitlam had asked to meet James to discuss the half-Senate election 'as a matter of courtesy', specifically the Liberal party federal council's 'incitement' of state Premiers to withhold writs, lamenting the Liberal party's repeated obstruction of convention and referring to the 24 previous occasions on which Senate writs had been issued by the state Governors.[70] Whitlam fully expected that if the Premiers advised their Governors not to issue writs then the Governors would act on that advice—consistent with his belief in the central tenet of Westminster parliamentary democracy that Governors and Governors-General act on the advice of their ministers. What is critical here, is that at no point during their conversation did Whitlam mention seeking the Queen's intervention in order to force the state Governors to issue the writs, much less propose it.

Nevertheless, the following day the British High Commission provided a confidential report to the FCO setting out the imagined scenario of Whitlam instructing the Governor-General to instruct the Queen on this matter. Their view, reached with the startling qualifier, 'without the benefit of any qualified or constitutional advice', was that 'this whole procedure ... is a constitutional impossibility'.[71] The 'whole procedure'—a refusal to issue writs and Whitlam instructing the Governor-General to instruct the Queen—was fanciful, a spectre entirely of their own making, built on little more than a rumour, a newspaper report and a decision of the Liberal party federal council. In adhering to this rumour as both fact and inevitability the High Commission was manifestly partisan, since its actions were to the direct political benefit of the Opposition which, as they knew, had everything to lose from the pending half-Senate election.

Hypotheticals and lack of 'any qualified legal and constitutional advice' notwithstanding, this speculation then led the High Commission to the extraordinary conclusion that 'We would expect that the Governor-General would decline to act on Mr Whitlam's advice, since he would presumably have to inform Mr Whitlam that he could not properly do so'.[72] That single sentence encapsulates the unerring sense of imperial privilege that underpins these archival records. The British High Commission in Canberra was proposing that the Governor-General, the Queen's representative, should break the cardinal rule of a constitutional monarchy—that the Crown acts on the advice of elected ministers—and not for any reason of illegality or unconstitutionality on the part of the Prime Minister whose advice it was to give, but in order to protect the Queen.[73] Its very articulation was a subversion of Australian democratic governance and political independence, and a denial of national sovereignty.

If this was not remarkable enough, what then transpired is astounding. The FCO sought to avert this confected 'crisis' of the states refusing to issue writs and its concomitant conflicting advice to the Queen by proposing its intervention in the half-Senate election, through the Governor-General, Sir John Kerr. It was Kerr who would have to act on the Prime Minister's advice to call the half-Senate election, Kerr who would set in train the issuing of writs for that election and it was Kerr whom the High Commission had already indicated would have to 'decline to act on Mr Whitlam's advice'. In a memo headed 'Australian domestic politics: possible intervention of UK government', the FCO took the High Commission's contemplated subversion of the half-Senate election even further. From its title alone this memo laid bare the unquestioned view in Whitehall that the UK could intervene in Australian domestic politics and that, if necessary, it would intervene. The only question was one of timing.

To this end, the FCO considered approaching Sir Martin Charteris to lean on Kerr to 'block off' the involvement of the Queen in the half-Senate election.[74] We know from Kerr's personal papers that he was in regular communication with Charteris at this time and that he received from

Charteris 'advice to me on dismissal'. Kerr had confided to both Charteris and Prince Charles in September 1975 his fear that Whitlam might try to recall him just as he was moving to dismiss the government. We also know that Charteris reassured Kerr that should that 'contingency' arise, the Palace would 'try to delay things', giving Kerr sufficient time to effect Whitlam's dismissal.[75] Kerr's official secretary, David Smith, has acknowledged that this secret communication between Charteris and Kerr took place in the weeks before the dismissal, in a breathtaking rupture of the vice-regal relationship.[76]

The constitutional essence of a constitutional monarchy is that the appointment of the Governor-General is made by the Queen of Australia on the advice of the Australian Prime Minister alone. For Charteris to intervene so clearly with Kerr himself in any prospective decision by Whitlam on the Governor-General's tenure was a shocking and subversive breach on every level. Kerr certainly took their secret communications not only as a

Royal green light for his continuing deception of Whitlam—after all, the Palace was doing the same—but as a Royal decree to do his 'duty' and protect the Queen. This extraordinary report, proposing outright intervention in the Australian electoral process through the Queen's private secretary, concludes that action by the FCO at that time, 21 October 1975, was too risky; 'Mr Whitlam, if he heard of it, would inevitably suspect the U.K.'s involvement. We should do nothing for the time being, except to continue to watch developments carefully'.

David Smith has conceded that protecting the Queen from involvement in the half-Senate election was the critical factor in Kerr's dismissal of Whitlam: 'Had the Governor-General accepted his Prime Minister's advice [to call the half-Senate election] and gone on to ask all state Governors to issue writs for the election of senators for their respective states, a refusal by even one state Governor to do so, let alone three, would have precipitated yet another kind of constitutional crisis.'[77] It was imperative that Kerr deny

Whitlam's advice to call the half-Senate election in order to avoid 'another kind of constitutional crisis', one that would involve the Queen in Whitlam's efforts to instruct the states.

The speculated 'crisis' emerging from the trifecta of hypotheticals—state Governors' refusing to issue writs, Whitlam instructing the Governor-General to instruct the Queen to instruct the Governors, and the Queen facing conflicting advice from Australian and British ministers—was now reduced to its immediate political imperative, preventing the half-Senate election. Given that the half-Senate election was both a constitutional requirement and due to be called by Whitlam at any time, there was only one way to prevent it—through the Governor-General. And since, as the FCO and even Kerr himself acknowledged, the Governor-General acts on the advice of the Prime Minister, the only means of preventing the half-Senate election would be to act before Whitlam had called it. These communications between the FCO and the High Commission proposing British intervention in Australian politics, centred on whether Kerr could be 'relied upon' to deal with the half-Senate election in such a way as to ensure that the Queen was not involved. They were left in no doubt that, 'certainly the Governor-General of Australia could be relied upon'.[78]

The 'reliability' of the Governor-General to do whatever was required in order to 'protect' the Queen would be checked and confirmed by the British High Commission and the FCO, and passed on to British ministers. A report from the FCO to the British High Commissioner in Canberra refers to the 'comforting confirmation' they had received of 'the view we had already expressed in submissions to Ministers that Sir John Kerr could be relied upon to resist any precipitant action that might involve either HM the Queen or HMG [Her Majesty's Government]'.[79] This report shows the extent of the deception and undermining of the Whitlam government as it moved towards the half-Senate election. As Whitlam prepared to call the half-Senate election he was completely unaware that the Governor-General 'could be relied upon' to meet his primary 'duty', as he saw it, to protect the Queen.

The FCO files also reveal that a critical meeting between Sir John Kerr and the most senior official in the FCO took place at this time. On 15 October 1975, the newly appointed Permanent Under-Secretary (designate) of the FCO, Sir Michael Palliser, arrived in Canberra on a whirlwind visit. The following day Palliser and the British High Commissioner, Sir Morrice James, travelled to Yarralumla for meetings with the Governor-General, just as Supply was being blocked in the Senate.[80] The files contain no record of these meetings between Kerr and two of the most senior British officials in the Australian–British relationship during the escalating political crisis. There is no report on it and no correspondence about it. A draft itinerary is all that remains to show that there had been any planned contact between the head of the FCO and the Queen's representative in Australia on such a significant day in our political history.

The day after his meeting with Kerr, Palliser held a second critical meeting, with the NSW Governor, Sir Roden Cutler. Cutler was an unusually significant player in the political intrigue then engulfing Canberra as he was due to stand in for Kerr, who was soon to leave on an official visit to the UK. Cutler and Kerr knew each other well and Kerr had previously, as Chief Justice of NSW, deputised for Cutler as Governor of NSW.[81] Recent events had made this vice-regal staff exchange rather more complicated and would place Cutler in an unexpectedly powerful position—he was to be acting as Governor-General (Administrator) while Supply was blocked in the Senate and as Whitlam moved to call the half-Senate election. There was something that Palliser needed to confirm before any of this could take place.

Palliser's meeting with Cutler focused entirely on the half-Senate election and its feared implications for the Queen. Palliser sought Cutler's view on whether Kerr would 'accede to a request from Whitlam ... to ask the Queen to instruct the Governors to call the election' (sic). Cutler reassured him that Kerr would not accept any request from Whitlam to ask the Queen to instruct the Governors—if that hypothetical scenario arose.[82]

But this was not the most important information to come from Palliser's meeting with Cutler. Even more critical was Cutler's view of the proprieties of vice-regal office. Unlike Kerr, Cutler strongly believed that as Governor he could act only on the advice of the elected minister, the Premier. In confirming to Palliser his view that Kerr was prepared to act against Whitlam's advice, Cutler at the same time made it clear that this was not his own view. Cutler told Palliser that if he was instructed by the Queen to act against his Premier's advice and issue the writs, he would resign rather than do so. For Palliser, Cutler's view of the vice-regal role was critical, for it was clear that as acting Governor-General during Kerr's planned absence in November, Cutler would act on Whitlam's advice and grant the half-Senate election. Indeed, Cutler has acknowledged that had he been acting as Governor-General on 11 November 1975, he 'would've done things differently'.[83]

Cutler held very different views from Kerr on the role of Governor-General and on the blocking of Supply. Cutler's view was that whatever happened in the Senate it was not the Governor-General's responsibility to resolve it, that the stalemate would be resolved in the parliament where some of the Senators were already showing signs of cracking. Kerr by contrast insisted to Cutler that, as Governor-General, he had to 'take control' of the situation, even though Supply had been blocked for just four days, and that it was critical he remain in the position as Governor-General, as 'he was the only one who really could carry it out'. The meeting between Palliser and Kerr had a history-defining corollary and immediately after it Kerr cancelled his planned November overseas trip, 'in order to keep his own hand on the tiller'.[84]

Kerr's decision to cancel his trip and remain in Australia was a turning point and yet as for so much in this historical drama there is no record of his critical meeting with Palliser among the files of the FCO. The continuing secrecy over these events more than forty years since the events themselves has left an insurmountable gap in the historical record and in our capacity to know our own history. Yet even these heavily redacted and security-stripped records consistently point to the stark conclusion of British involvement in the dismissal of the Whitlam government.

On 11 November 1975, Kerr dismissed Whitlam, just as the Prime Minister was handing him the agreed written advice to call the half-Senate election. Kerr always insisted that by dismissing Whitlam he had met his 'duty to the Monarch' and had protected the Queen by ensuring that she had not 'become involved in our crisis'.[85] There is no doubt that this essentially British imperative, of protecting the Queen, was a critical factor in Kerr's decision to dismiss the Whitlam government.[86] Yet the dismissal served only to achieve the opposite effect, drawing the Queen into exceptional political controversy over the Governor-General's invocation of archaic prerogative powers in the name of the Crown. The controversy was further fuelled by the dramatic partisan impact of Kerr's action on the respective electoral chances of the government and Opposition, in which the Queen's representative appeared neither neutral nor disinterested. As the British High Commissioner acknowledged; 'Rarely can the fortunes of a major political party in a Western democracy have been so dramatically reversed'.[87]

Far from playing the role of imperial guide and protector of its own Westminster style democracy among its former colonies, the fading colonial power had intervened in Australian domestic politics and interfered in the democratic process of a member of its own Commonwealth. Other Commonwealth nations were equally alarmed by Kerr's revival of the prerogative powers, with its obvious implications for their national autonomy. The FCO quickly damped down the concerns of the President of Sierra Leone, with an imperious reminder of the 'correct' position—that this was solely an Australian matter in which 'it would not be proper' for the Queen to be involved.[88] Kerr's actions also sent shock waves through the British Labour government of Prime Minister, Harold Wilson, with some party members calling for a review of the prerogative powers. An internal Labour party paper circulated just weeks after the dismissal, insisted that the power to remove a government and to dissolve parliament must rest only with the Parliament, asserting parliamentary sovereignty over any claimed vestigial power of the Crown.[89]

This fundamental incompatibility between independent parliamentary government and an unarticulated residual power of the Crown remains the contradiction at the heart of Australia as a constitutional monarchy. The disjuncture between protecting British self-interest and upholding Australian parliamentary democracy can never be resolved until Australia becomes a fully independent Republic with an Australian Head of State.

Only one thing can address the disturbing questions that arise from this damaging episode in British–Australian relations, and that is a full joint inquiry into the nature and extent of British involvement in the dismissal of the Whitlam government. Although we now know so much more about the dismissal, with each new piece in the puzzle painstakingly emerging from interviews, original sources and archival revelations, the most important documents are closed to us just as they have been for more than forty years. Like recalcitrant colonial children, we still cannot be trusted with such a dangerous thing as knowledge of our own history. An inquiry into British involvement that can call for the release of documents from the UK National Archives and the National Archives of Australia, the files of the FCO, the British High Commission and material in the Royal Archives, will finally tell us what really happened on 11 November 1975.

It is time for the deception to end.

7

'THE MAN WHO WOULD BE KING'

'That the King can do no wrong is a necessary and fundamental principle of the English constitution.' [1]

William Blackstone

FOR EACH OF the three protagonists—Gough Whitlam, Malcolm Fraser and Sir John Kerr—the impact of the dismissal was absolute. For Whitlam it was the end of a government he had spent over twenty years in Opposition working to achieve, and the effective end of his political career; for Fraser it was the beginning of seven years as Prime Minister, and the start of a remaking of himself and his history that would later see him turn his back on the Liberal party and brazenly claim a unity with the policies of the Whitlam government. For Sir John Kerr it was simply the beginning of the end.

Always a vain, insecure, needy man, with an alarming taste for alcohol, the dismissal would define Kerr, eclipsing all else in his long legal career and marking a point of rapid personal decline. His was a particularly cruel end, and it began at once. Just hours after dismissing Whitlam, the Governor-General dined at Yarralumla with his usual entourage of staff, David Smith and Lady Kerr, and that day there were also three visiting servicemen, candidates for the position of *aidede-camp.* One of these, Bill Denny, recalled Kerr arriving late to lunch and announcing dramatically, 'I've sacked your Prime Minister; I've put another one in his place. God help us all'.[2] Having already partaken of gin and tonic at pre-lunch drinks before dismissing Whitlam, Kerr 'imbibed freely', telling the assembled party 'this occasion probably warrants a drink or two'.[3]

Over lunch, punctuated by strained conversation, Kerr 'swung to extremes', darting between topics and sinking into maudlin self-reflection. He shocked the young guests by asking them—his junior job applicants—whether he had made the right decision in dismissing Whitlam; 'he was vacillating ... "I don't know if I made the right decision"'.[4] What struck them all was that the Governor-General was not 'the forceful man we had expected'.[5] The improbable scene continued at dinner, where Denny was seated next to a 'visibly intoxicated' Governor-General: 'It was red wine, he'd grab it, throwing down a big mouthful'.[6] Kerr had begun a descent into self-doubt, recrimination and obsession with the dismissal that, perversely, only intensified over time.

Fraser had recognised Kerr's critical weakness in his need for political and legal affirmation, his sense of inferiority and self-doubt, and had exploited it ruthlessly as Fraser himself later acknowledged.[7] That was Kerr's tragedy. To Fraser, Kerr was a weak man, easily manipulated to action and readily suborned with approbation and honorifics. Soon after assuming government, Fraser reprised aspects of the imperial honours system, reintroducing Knights and Dames, which had been scrapped by Whitlam and replaced by the introduction of the Australian honours system. The first of Fraser's newly revived Knighthoods included just two recipients, Sir John Kerr and Sir Robert Menzies. In May 1976 Kerr became the first Knight in the newly created Knight of the Order of Australia.

Imperial recognition began within days of the dismissal, when Kerr received a personal letter of support for his 'courageous and correct' actions from the Queen's cousin, Lord Louis Mountbatten.[8] This was a remarkably partisan intercession from such a major royal figure and Mountbatten followed it up with a private visit to Admiralty House early the following year. Coming from a senior member of the royal family, Mountbatten's letter to Kerr so soon after the dismissal would be of great interest and could shed some light on just what the Palace knew. This letter should now be open for public access as part of Kerr's papers in the National Archives of Australia and yet, like the Palace letters, it is not. A series of previously unpublished letters between Kerr and Smith, revealed here for the first time, tells us why. It paints a disturbing picture of Government House carelessness at best, and destruction of official records at worst, involving a cleaner, a trolley and the Yarralumla incinerator.

Kerr was clearly impressed by the royal sentiments expressed in Mountbatten's letter, describing it as being 'of outstanding value to me', and soon after leaving office he asked Smith to send a copy to him. A rather nervous Smith prevaricated for some weeks before finally telling Kerr that he could not send Mountbatten's letter—because it had been burnt. According to this improbable story, an overzealous cleaner had accidentally placed a box of letters, including Mountbatten's, on a trolley destined for the Yarralumla incinerator. Had Lord Mountbatten's letter survived its unintended incineration it would now be part of the wealth of material among Kerr's papers in the Archives that has proved so invaluable in unravelling the hidden history of the dismissal. Smith was well aware of the significance of Mountbatten's letter and the implications of its destruction, expressing his 'deep regret that, despite my efforts to preserve all of these letters as part of the archives of this office, they should have been lost in this way'.[9]

Six weeks after the dismissal, Kerr arrived in London for an audience with the Queen. There was lunch and dinner with the Queen at Sandringham in January 1976, and a personal invitation to attend Morning Service with her at Sandringham Church.[10] In March 1977 during her visit to Australia, the Queen bestowed on Kerr the highest order of her personal honour, Knight Grand Cross of the Royal Victorian Order, which recognises 'personal service to the Monarchy' and is 'entirely within the Sovereign's personal gift'. These were hardly signs of royal dismay at the Governor-General's unprecedented action in dismissing the twice-elected Whitlam government without warning, as some journalists have since claimed.[11]

The Queen had been kept regularly informed by Kerr in the weeks before the dismissal of his view of unfolding events and was well aware of the prospect that he might move to dismiss

Whitlam in a quasi-colonial mutation of 'the divine right of Kings'. Far from expressing concern at this possibility—either by warning Whitlam of it or urging Kerr against it—the few comments from Palace officials since have never demurred from Kerr's action, but have merely suggested that the Governor-General acted too soon.[12] Their only concern about the dismissal appears to have been one of timing.

It is simply astonishing to read the continuing efforts to recast this now clear element in the history of the dismissal as its opposite—to claim that the Palace was somehow embarrassed by Kerr's action in dismissing Whitlam and even disagreed with it.[13] All the evidence shows us otherwise. Indeed in his private papers Kerr writes that he offered his resignation to the Palace immediately after the dismissal, which the Palace opposed.[14] Although Kerr has been portrayed as determined not to involve the Queen in the events of 1975, his actions did precisely that. From the moment he first raised with the Palace the possibility of dismissal,

Kerr had interposed the Palace directly in his decision.

The official accolades for Kerr's 'personal service' to Australia and 'service to the Monarchy' did little to disguise the depth of feeling that remained towards him for dismissing Whitlam in such deceptive circumstances and appointing Fraser as Prime Minister, despite his lack of a majority in the House of Representatives. Both Fraser and Kerr hoped that the initial outcry over the dismissal, the infuriated and infuriating demonstrators, the blockades and the pungent criticisms would soon cease, that they would fade into the political background and be quickly forgotten, and that politics could somehow resume its rightful order. But from the opening of the new Parliament in 1976, boycotted by every Labor member and with Kerr addressing a depleted chamber, the protests continued unabated. For the next twelve months angry crowds with megaphones, banners and placards confronted Kerr at every outing, blocking paths, pounding doors, hurling insults and reminding the Fraser government and

Kerr of what they simply wanted to forget. Kerr termed it, rather grandiosely, 'the battle of the streets'.[15]

The Melbourne Scots' annual St Andrew's Day dinner one year after the dismissal brought welcome relief. A bastion of Melbourne establishment conservatism, the Prime Minister, Malcolm Fraser, was a special guest at the dinner and Kerr attended as a guest of the Melbourne Scots' revered former president, Sir Robert Menzies. Menzies proposed a toast to the Governor-General, a man 'of superb distinction and character', and as Kerr rose to speak the room erupted.[16] In an overtly partisan display, details of which were not intended for public release, Kerr's every word was greeted with cheers, accolades and expressions of exuberant gratitude.[17] Former Liberal party leader Billy Snedden recalled the extraordinary scene as the Governor-General departed, drunk and swaying on his feet. Kerr raised his hands above his head as he staggered to the door, clasping them in victory, 'like a boxer just having won the crown ... It sickened me'.[18]

By 1977 Kerr's behaviour had become too erratic, too public and too embarrassing even for Fraser to continue to indulge his excesses. Front-page headlines such as that in the Melbourne *Age,* 'A cow of a day for Kerr', did little to help the perception of an untenable Governor-General protected by and in turn protecting the Fraser government.[19] The story began, 'The Governor-General, Sir John Kerr, fell to the ground after a cow stood on his foot at the Tamworth Show at the week-end'. Kerr had just placed the Champion Dairy Cow ribbon around the ample neck of the appropriately named 'Lovedale Posh', when 'the cow lifted its leg and put it down firmly on the side of Sir John's shoe'. There the Governor-General remained, flat on his back and pinioned under Lovedale Posh's back left hoof as Lady Kerr tried to move the beast away from the prostrate Viceroy. When local Tamworth photographer Paul Mathews won the Walkley Award for best photograph later that year, he brought the house down with the rather ambiguous line, 'and last but not least, I'd like to thank the cow'.[20]

The alcohol-fuelled trajectory that had landed Kerr prone in the mud at the Tamworth Show was merely the precursor to his most dramatic public appearance at the Melbourne Cup some months later. There, in the glorious absurdity of his ill-fitting top hat and tails much loved of cartoonists and which came to epitomise Kerr, he gave a repeat performance, swaying through the crowd as he approached the dais, well primed by drinks with the Governor of Victoria Sir Henry Winneke before the race and with former Premier Sir Henry Bolte during it.[21] Although this time the Governor-General remained largely upright as he struggled to award the Cup to the owners of the winning horse, the usual hecklers agitated him and most unwisely Kerr responded, slurring, 'Ladies and gentlemen, any noises that you may happen to hear are only static. It's just something wrong with the system'. Whitlam was moved to consider, 'how much better a pro-consul the horse would have made'.[22] Kerr was at risk of becoming little more than a favoured punchline.

It is hardly surprising that the Queen, in whose name Kerr officially acted, eventually joined the long list of those who by mid-1977 were hoping the Governor-General would make a hasty early retirement. The prospect of Kerr's resignation had been considered for some time, and Fraser initially had insisted that Kerr remain, concerned that his resignation would only make things worse, that it would cast doubt on Kerr's own view of the correctness of the dismissal. Kerr agreed; he had no intention of resigning, believing that it would 'bring into question the legitimacy of my decision' to dismiss Whitlam and that 'a Governor-General who had properly exercised the reserve power could not be driven from office'.[23]

However as Kerr, the office of Governor-General, and increasingly the monarchy itself, were damaged by the ramifications of the dismissal and by Kerr's continuing personal dissolution, Kerr was under enormous pressure. Early in 1977 he began extensive negotiations with Fraser over ways in which he could, in his words, 'be of further service to Australia'. The obvious answer, 'by resigning', was to Kerr an admission of personal failure and political error and at first he refused to contemplate it. Finally, in July 1977, it was announced that Kerr would resign as Governor-General at the end of the year. The ten-year term that he had insisted on before accepting the position from Whitlam, had lasted just three years.

Soon after this announcement, Kerr contacted Harry M Miller, 'agent to the stars', and who was later to serve time in Long Bay jail for fraud.[24] Kerr was planning to move to London and to write his memoirs, his account of the dismissal of the Whitlam government that would correct 'the bogus history, falsehood and invention' swirling around him.[25] Miller became his agent, negotiating fees for personal appearances, media interviews, serial rights and royalties on a book that was expected to generate 'substantial income' estimated by Miller, with typical agent's flair, at between $350,000 and $500,000.

Money was a longstanding concern for Kerr; it had been the root of the inordinate delay in his decision to accept the position of Governor-General in 1974, for which he would stand down as Chief Justice of the NSW Supreme Court after just eighteen months. Kerr had kept Whitlam and government officials busy for months as he sought not only the unprecedented ten-year term but also a 50 per cent increase in the Governor-General's salary; an additional payment to cover lost superannuation; 'outfitting allowances' for himself and Lady Kerr; and a pension on retirement. And now, in perfect symmetry as he faced his reluctant departure, it was money that again occupied him.

Kerr's major concern was tax. Specifically, that he would have to pay it. With the income tax threshold at 60 per cent for the top-tier income range, he was looking at paying additional tax of between $210,000 and $300,000 on projected book earnings. Miller then contacted the chartered accountants

Greenwood Challoner & Co, who in turn wrote to the law firm of Allen Allen & Hemsley (Allens), well versed in problematic large-scale tax matters, to address the unfortunate prospect of the Governor-General's tax. The key to Kerr's predicament was identified by Greenwood Challoner from the outset: if the income is earned in Australia then tax must be paid, the challenge therefore was to find a way to avoid income from the book being seen as earned in Australia. However, and this was the rub, if Kerr entered into acceptable arrangements with an 'offshore entity' based in a 'designated tax haven' in order to minimise his tax, the Reserve Bank of Australia must first approve those arrangements as ones that 'did not involve the evasion of ... Australian tax'.[26] This then was the central dilemma, that in order to obtain a tax clearance certificate from the Reserve Bank of Australia confirming that no tax evasion was involved, both the tax avoidance and the tax avoider would have to be identified, and Kerr wanted neither.

Other, more opaque schemes were available to avoid this unwanted disclosure and identification which, as Greenwood Challoner discreetly put it, 'in the normal course they would recommend' to Miller's client. However, Greenwood Challoner recognised what Kerr himself did not—that his position as Governor-General might lead him to pause before taking such a questionable path: 'This matter is, however, somewhat delicate and we suggest that your client might wish to obtain further advice from Senior Counsel before he made his decision'.[27]   Twice Greenwood Challoner sounded a note of caution, a hint of the ethical dilemma that Miller's client, 'in view of his present position', ought to consider before setting on a path to avoid the requirements of the Reserve Bank of Australia. And twice these admonitions of ethical and possibly legal breaches went unheeded.[28]

Allens showed no such hesitation. Their concern was not Kerr's position, but his identity. In their view it was 'most desirable' that Kerr keep his identity hidden and on a need-to-know basis.[29] Throughout these negotiations Sir John Kerr was Governor-General of Australia and holding the Oath of Office of Governor-General in which he had sworn to 'do right to all manner of people after the laws and usages of the Commonwealth of Australia'. What transpired was a moment when law and ethics collided and, once again, Kerr's judgement was lacking. For the purposes of these negotiations on tax avoidance and financial matters, Kerr chose secrecy over transparency, self-interest over propriety, and a dereliction of his Oath of Office to 'do right' after the laws of Australia. The Governor-General adopted a pseudonym, and the name he chose was remarkable in its resonance and its association—Sir John Kerr became 'Mr Frederick King'.

For the next three months Frederick King and Allens deliberated on a scheme that would effectively subvert the usual oversight of the Governor-General's financial dealings by the Reserve Bank of Australia and so avoid both disclosure and tax. Allens had a legal pedigree stretching back to the 1820s and an equally long history of involvement with and legal support for the conservative side of politics. Its alumni included former Prime Minister Billy McMahon, High Court justices and several New South Wales and Victorian Supreme Court judges. They had retained Sir Garfield Barwick QC as lead counsel for the Bankers' Association in 1948 in the Bank Nationalisation case against the Chifley government's legislation to nationalise the private banks. Allens had again provided legal advice for the Bankers' Association during the term of the Whitlam government.

During the 1980s, at the height of the Hawke government's efforts to crack down on tax evasion, Allens was under great pressure from the Tax Office to allow it to conduct a full audit of their clients' trust account records, against which they repeatedly claimed legal professional privilege. In 1988 the Deputy Commissioner of Taxation took action against Allens in the Federal Court, claiming misuse of 'client privilege' and seeking the release of those documents. They succeeded on every point. As the case progressed, Fred Lind, one of the partners at Allens, gave some insight into the expansive and convenient idea of what constituted 'privilege': 'Privilege is like a horse: you know one when you see one'.[30] And Allens saw a lot of horses that year. The Tax Office's pursuit was led by the redoubtable, relentless auditor Bob 'Bulldog' Fitton. Asked whether he considered Allens to be a reputable firm of solicitors, Fitton replied: 'From my point of view, no ... They were giving more than just legal advice, they were actually encouraging people to engage in activities that were most immoral in my opinion'.[31]

In the end, Allens proposed a highly complex scheme for Mr King, involving a tangle of companies across two countries, with documents to be signed in a third country. It was known as an 'Uncle Charlie' scheme and included a trust in the United Kingdom, a company in the Netherlands, a second company in the United Kingdom, and necessitated a trip to Hong Kong, where 'Mr King' would sign the necessary documents.[32] Through the company transfers, sales, sublicensing and assignments of rights and capital, Kerr's earnings would be offshore and minimal, and neither the Reserve Bank of Australia nor the Australian Tax Office would know anything about it. Allens advised that the UK company that would hold the copyright in Kerr's book was Aprolon Limited. Kerr's memoirs, *Matters for Judgment,* were released the following year and specified on the title page is the copyright holder, Aprolon Limited. Kerr ended his term as Governor-General on 8 December 1977, just one week after the incorporation of Aprolon Limited with a registered address in Jermyn Street, London.[33]

On 9 December Kerr was on his way to London via Hong Kong, carrying instructions from Allens to their Hong Kong contact, Mr Carter, that read more like a script for a B-grade thriller than a message from a recently retired Governor-General:

Mr Frederick King and his wife are arriving in Hong Kong on Saturday 10 December and will be staying at the Peninsula Hotel. Mr King will have with him:

1. Three Powers of Attorney in favour of yourself;

2. Three deeds of Agreement in duplicate;

3. A letter from me to you with instructions.

I have told Mr King that you will telephone him at the Peninsula Hotel first thing on Monday morning with a view to calling upon him to collect Powers of Attorney and ... for the purpose of executing the various agreements in accordance with the instructions contained in my letter to you.[34]

Carter was one of only two people, according to Allens, aware of the identity of Mr King. 'Apart from these two persons it has not been necessary and will not be necessary, to disclose Your Excellency's identity and this we believe is most desirable.'[35] The benefits of this structure for Mr King were clearly set out: it would avoid having to seek the authority of the Reserve Bank of Australia; the provisions of the Banking (Foreign Exchange) Regulations would have no application; it would avoid having to make any disclosure of King's interest in his Australian income tax returns;

and only minimal taxation would be payable.[36] It was a triumph of legal chicanery over personal, and vice-regal, propriety. A further benefit was that the entire trip—first-class airfares and one week's accommodation for Kerr and his wife—was financed by the Australian taxpayer, a parting gift approved by Malcolm Fraser, 'as a farewell call on the Queen'.[37]

Through all these negotiations, Kerr had been intending to leave Australia as soon as he had resigned and relocate to England, where he would 'establish a residence in London'.[38] Indeed much of the tax avoidance contrivance options had been devised with that location in mind. But then, just three weeks before he was due to leave Australia, Kerr's plans appeared to have been upended when Allens advised him that their carefully designed scheme might not succeed if he was to live in London. This critical fact, no small matter for Mr King, had apparently only just 'emerged' from Allens' UK consultants, who had advised that 'Mr King should take care that no part of his activities in writing the book takes place within the United Kingdom'. Otherwise, British tax laws might yet take from Kerr the very tax he had worked so hard to preserve. It was *essential,* Allens concluded, that Mr King write his book 'outside the United Kingdom—say, in France'.[39]

In alerting Kerr to the problem, Allens had also pointed to the solution and it soon became clear that the Paris option for Mr King was no moot point. Kerr had been away from Australia for two months and, as the furore over his term in office subsided with the popular appointment of his successor, Governor-General Sir Zelman Cowen, it no doubt seemed a good time for Fraser to make the stunning announcement that he did on 9 February 1978. In a quietly worded press release, Fraser announced the appointment of the former Governor-General, Sir John Kerr, as Australia's Ambassador to UNESCO, stating that he regarded Kerr as 'admirably qualified for the post'. The position would begin in just three weeks and, most importantly, it would be based in Paris.[40]

The extraordinary revelations from Kerr's private papers of his arduous tax negotiations in the name of Mr King present yet another element in the troubled history of the dismissal, its aftermath, and the relationship between its key players. It profoundly challenges our previous understanding of the circumstances of Kerr's appointment to UNESCO, given his lawyers' advice that he locate himself 'say, in France'. Certainly what appeared to be a sudden and unexpected offer of Ambassador provided the Paris option already flagged by Allens as the necessary solution to Mr King's tax avoidance dilemma. Quite apart from the choice of Kerr as Ambassador, this was a remarkable appointment since the position of Australia's Ambassador to UNESCO no longer existed. Fraser had abolished it two years earlier as an austerity measure, only for it now to be re-established in what Clyde Cameron described as 'the resurrection of a sinecure'.[41]

The outcry was immediate, predictable and visceral. Labor leader Bill Hayden condemned it as 'an affront to this country', future Labor Prime Minister Paul Keating accused Fraser of 'buying off a Governor-General', and even Fraser's cabinet was deeply divided over the appointment.[42] But it was Senator Jim McClelland's vicious parliamentary commentary on his one-time friend turned 'vulgar race-course drunk', devastating in its cruelty and precise in its insight, that stung Kerr the most.[43] Kerr arrived in Paris on 1 March and, in his first and only action as Ambassador to UNESCO, resigned.[44] In one of the wonderful ironies of history, Gough Whitlam was appointed in 1983 to the position of Australia's Ambassador to UNESCO by the Hawke government. Whitlam's experience as Australia's Ambassador could not have been more different, and at the end of his three-year term, he was elected as a member of the Executive Board of UNESCO for four years.[45]

Despite the repeated denials by Fraser and Kerr of any prior discussion between them concerning the UNESCO position, the appearance of a sinecure was unavoidable. Specifically, that Kerr's resignation as Governor-General in 1977 had been predicated on the offer of the UNESCO position and that this had been discussed much earlier than either would admit. Neither Ayres' biography of Fraser nor Fraser's own jointly penned memoirs enlighten us further on the UNESCO appointment, since both books deal with this whole episode in a single sentence.[46] Following the announcement of Kerr's appointment, Fraser was asked the crucial question directly in the House of Representatives, in a question without notice from Keating: 'On what date did he [Fraser] first discuss with Sir John Kerr a further government appointment for him in the event of his retirement as Governor-General?' In response Fraser could not have been clearer, telling the parliament that the offer of the UNESCO position had been put to Kerr, 'very shortly before the announcement was actually made'.[47]

Kerr publicly adopted the same timeline, insisting that he had not discussed the UNESCO position with Fraser at the time of his resignation as Governor-General. In *Matters for*

Judgment, Kerr describes the offer as entirely unexpected, a 'dramatic interruption' to his holiday that necessitated the abandoning of his planned move to London.[48] Indeed, Kerr reserved his sharpest invective, his bitterest and most aggrieved admonishment, against any suggestion that his appointment to the UNESCO position was in any way linked to his resignation as Governor-General. It would have been, he claimed, 'entirely inconsistent with my character ... There is not a spark of truth in it'. Kerr asserted indignantly and, it seems, unwisely that: 'History will confirm its truth when the time comes for the related documents to be published'.[49]

That time has come and those documents have now been released. A series of previously unpublished letters from Kerr's private papers shows Fraser and Kerr's insistence that they had no prior discussion about the UNESCO position to be simply untrue.[50] On 8 July 1977, one week before the announcement of his forthcoming resignation as Governor-General, Kerr was sent a draft of Fraser's statement announcing the resignation, by the Head of the Department of Prime Minister and Cabinet, Geoff Yeend. Several amendments have been written directly onto the draft in Kerr's own hand, and a copy of the draft with Kerr's annotations remains in the file. In all, Kerr proposed nine amendments, one of which was this critical sentence: *'The Australian Government is pleased to announce his appointment as Australian Ambassador to UNESCO'.* The amendments were discussed with Yeend and, through Yeend, with Fraser. All but two of Kerr's amendments were then included in the final statement released by Fraser on 14 July 1977; the reference to Kerr's UNESCO appointment was not among them.[51]

Contrary to his and Fraser's public assertions, Kerr clearly knew of his appointment to the UNESCO position at the time of his resignation as Governor-General and had expected it would be announced at the same time as his resignation. Yet he and Fraser repeatedly denied that any such appointment had even been discussed at that time. In his reply to Keating's question without notice about the timing of his discussions with Kerr on the appointment, Fraser had simply continued the now ritualistic dissembling about every contested aspect of the dismissal and its repercussions. In doing so he misled the Australian parliament, the Australian people, and our history.

The real story of the dismissal has emerged over decades, pieced together from a series of revelations in which each of the key protagonists, and some we had never imagined, left a record of their role. In this historical correction, no single holding has proved more significant than Kerr's papers, held by the National Archives of Australia. From the revelations of Sir Anthony Mason's role, the limited details of Kerr's communications with the Palace, Mr King's tax dealings, to the full story of Kerr's appointment to UNESCO, Kerr's archives have been critical to the reassessment of the history of the dismissal. Yet what is remarkable, and alarming, is just how close we came to those papers never being opened to us.

The lodging of Kerr's papers with the Archives straddled two critical events—the March 1983 election, which saw the defeat of the Fraser government and the election of the Hawke government, and the passage of the *Archives Act.* One of the Fraser government's Bills still before the parliament at the time of the 1983 election was the Archives Bill. With Fraser's defeat, the Archives Bill was slightly but significantly revised and re-presented in 1983 by the Hawke government. A critical change was this: the Archives Bill as proposed by the Fraser government did not apply to 'records of the Governor-General', whereas the *Archives Act* passed under Hawke gave no such exemption to the records of Governors-General. Had the Archives Bill as originally proposed by the Fraser government prevailed, none of the dramatic and historic revelations from Kerr's papers, which have so significantly recast the dismissal, would be known today. Even Kerr's secret interactions with High Court Justice Sir Anthony Mason, now recognised as central to that history, could still be hidden and Mason's role protected.[52]

Although we are now much clearer on the reality of that exceptional episode, one key element remains hidden, as deliberately and as carefully concealed as every other aspect has been in this blighted history. This is 'the Palace letters'—letters between the Governor-General and the Queen, her private secretary Sir Martin Charteris, and Prince Charles—in the months leading up to Kerr's dismissal of Whitlam. Kerr's papers in the Archives were opened for public access, as required after thirty years since the date of their creation. But not the Palace letters. Unlike any other items in these papers, Kerr's correspondence with the Palace is embargoed until 2027. Even once this embargo has been lifted, these letters will only be released if authorised by the Queen's Private Secretary—a humiliating deference given the quasi-colonial relationship this whole matter reflects.

How has this extraordinary situation come about? The answer is very simple, and it has just two words, 'personal' and 'private'. With that simple designation, personal and private, the

Palace letters have been removed from the reach of the *Archives Act* and the usual thirty-year access provisions do not apply. Instead, personal and private records operate according to their own specific conditions of access. Revelations from Kerr's papers indicate that the specific access conditions placed on the Palace letters were set not by Kerr but by the official secretary, David Smith, in consultation with the Palace and 'in accordance with the Queen's wishes'.[53]

In 2027, more than fifty years after the dismissal of the Whitlam government, we will still be beholden to the Queen as to whether the Australian public can access this vital correspondence between Australia's Governor-General and the Palace, during one of the most contentious and significant episodes in our political history. There could be no better example of our arcane and subservient status as a constitutional monarchy than this—that we cannot know the full history of the dismissal of the Whitlam government until the Queen says we can.

POSTSCRIPT

FORTY YEARS LATER, the truth about the dismissal has emerged in moments—an accidental slip-up, a retributional revelation, an unguarded admission—slowly building a picture as the pieces converged. The image is not an honourable one. Although the history of the dismissal as we now understand it appears almost unrecognisable from the obscured and refracted story presented in the days that followed Kerr's actions in 1975, the full story continues to elude us.

The gradual, resisted discovery of this story was almost as shocking as the story itself. As it unfolded, recasting the history of key incidents, passionate positions and long-held presumptions, it also unmasked the coldly calculated decisions of men at the peak of public office determined to keep their actions hidden from the public, to allow the distortions of history to take shape and to continue unchallenged. If the dismissal is the political story that keeps on giving, it is because it is steeped in this deception. At every stage it required deception—in its inception, in its implementation and, after the dismissal, in its telling. The dismissal was never a matter of law, not even a matter of politics alone, but of personal and political choices, of ethics and of morals.

NOTES

PROEM

[1] Menadue, J, 'Note for File', *Double Dissolution of Parliament 11 November 1975,* Department of Prime Minister and Cabinet, 12 November 1975, National Archives of Australia (NAA) A1209 1975/2448; Smith, D, *Head of State: The Governor-General, the Monarchy, the Republic and the Dismissal,* MacLeay Press, Sydney, 2005, p.243.

[2] *PM,* ABC Radio program, 11 November 1975, http://whitlamdi smissal.com/1975/11/11/lunchtim e-on-november-11.html (accessed 31 July 2015).

[3] The Country party had changed its name to National Country party earlier that year. The Coalition Senators voted to defer consideration of the Appropriation Bills, 'until the Government agrees to submit itself to the judgment of the people'.

[4]   There was a slight possibility that the unique circumstance of the lower half-Senate quota, the two replacement Senators in Queensland and NSW together with the election of four first-time Territory Senators, might see the Whitlam government gain control of the Senate for six months, until the new Senators took their places in July 1976.

[5]   'Fraser Appeal at All Time Low', *The Bulletin,* 8 November 1975, pp.14–15; *Melbourne Herald,* 14 November 1975, p.4.

[6]   Kerr, JR, 'Letter of Dismissal from Governor-General Sir John Kerr to the Prime Minister, the Honourable Edward Gough Whitlam', 11 November 1975, NAA, http://www .naa.gov.au/collection/snapshots/d ismissal/dismissal-letter.aspx (accessed 29 July 2015).

[7]   *Commonwealth of Australia Constitution Act,* s.62, 63; Parliament of Australia Infosheet 20, 'The Australian System of Government', www.aph.gov.au/Ab out_Parliament/House_of_Represe

ntatives/ (accessed 2 August 2015).

[8] Kerr, JR, 'Notes on the Conspiracy and Deceit Theory', personal and confidential papers of Sir John Kerr, notes and papers on the constitutional crisis of 1975 and the political events that followed, NAA M4524 2005 Item 6; Kerr, JR, *Matters for Judgment: An Autobiography,* Macmillan, Melbourne, 1978, p.355.

[9] Lloyd, C, and A Clark, *Kerr's King Hit!,* Cassell Australia, Sydney, 1976, p.232; Kelly, P, *The Unmaking of Gough,* Allen & Unwin, Sydney, 1994, p.294; Ayres, P, *Malcolm Fraser: A Biography,* William Heinemann Australia, Melbourne, 1987, pp.292–3.

[10] 'New Evidence Supports Fraser 1975 Claim', *Canberra Times,* 28 November 1987, cited in Hefner, R, and P Malone, *Canberra Times,* 28 November 1987, p.1.

[11] 'Secret: Cabinet Meeting 11 November 1975', Records of the

Cabinet Office, United Kingdom National Archives, CM (72) 36.

[12] Charteris, M, to Scholes, G, 17 November 1975, 'Letter from the Queen's Private Secretary', Dismissal Documents, http://whi tlamdismissal.com/1975/11/17/le tter-from-queensprivate-secretar y.html (accessed 17 July 2015).

[13] Kerr, JR, 'Statement of Reasons', 11 November 1975, 'Letter from the Queen's Private Secretary', Dismissal Documents, http://whi tlamdismissal.com/1975/11/11/k err-statement-of-reasons.html (accessed 17 July 2015).

[14] In Benns, M, 'November 11 1975: Gough Whitlam's Final Kerr-tain', *The Daily Telegraph,* 22 October 2014.

[15] Whitlam, EG, interview in *Queen and Country* (dir. William Shawcross), BBC Television, 2002.

1. WHAT DID THE PALACE KNOW?

[1] Kerr, JR, *Matters for Judgment,* p.330.

[2] Hocking, J, *Gough Whitlam: His Time,* pp.264–5.

[3] Kerr, JR, 1980 Journal, 1 Part 17, p.6.

[4] Kerr, JR, 1980 Journal, (my emphasis), p.137.

[5] Kerr, JR, *Matters for Judgment,* p.358.

[6] Queckett, M, 'No wake-up call for the Queen over dismissal', *The West Australian,* April 2011. Dismissal Documents, http://whitl amdismissal.com/tag/william-hesel tine (accessed 17 July 2015).

[7] Denny, B in Hocking, J, *Gough Whitlam: His Time,* p.335; Smith, D, 'Sir David Smith, Dale Budd and the Dismissal', *Sydney Institute Quarterly* 9 (4), January 2006, pp.21–2; 22.

[8] Whitlam, EG, *The Truth of the Matter,* p.110.

[9] Kerr, JR, 1980 Journal, Private Papers of Sir John Kerr, NAA M4523, 1 Part 17.

[10] Kirby, M, in Dellora, D, *Michael Kirby: Law, Love & Life,* Penguin Books, Melbourne, 2012, p.184.

[11] Dimbleby, J, *The Prince of Wales,* Little, Brown & Co, London, 1994, p.226.

[12] Kerr, JR, to the Prince of Wales, 'Your Royal Highness', 25 February 1981 NAA M4526; Kerr, JR, to the Prince of Wales, 'Your Royal Highness', 7 November 1981, NAA M4526.

[13] Kerr, JR, 1980 Journal, p.17.

[14] Kerr, JR, Miscellaneous Handwritten Notes, Private Papers of Sir John Kerr, NAA M4523, 1 Part 16.

[15] 'No Wake-up Call for the Queen over Dismissal', *The West Australian,* April 2011 in Queckett, M, Dismissal Documents, http://whitlamdismissal.com/tag/william-heseltine (accessed 17 July 2015). (My emphasis.)

[16] Kerr, J, in Oakes, L, *Crash Through or Crash: The Unmaking of a Prime Minister,* Drummond, Melbourne, 1976, p.205.

2. WHAT DID THE HIGH COURT JUSTICE(S) KNOW?

[1] Barwick, G, to Kerr, J, 10 November 1975, NAA M4526, 4 Part 1.

[2] Garfield Barwick, Oral History Interview, NLA TRC 3317.

[3] Barwick, G, *Sir John Did His Duty,* Serendip Publications, Wahroonga, 1983, p.80.

[4] Barwick, G, *A Radical Tory: Reflections and Recollections,* Federation Press, Sydney, 1995, p.298.

[5] Barwick, G, Letter to the Governor-General, Sir John Kerr, 10 November 1975, 'Sir Garfield Barwick's Advice to Sir John Kerr', http://whitlamdismissal.com/1975 /11/10/barwick-advice-to-kerr.htm l (accessed 19 August 2015).

[6] Barwick, G, Address to the National Press Club, 10 June 1976, NLA ORAL TRC4042.

[7] Marr, D, *Barwick: The Classic Biography of a Man of Power,* Allen & Unwin, Sydney, 1992 (1980), pp.xi–xii.

[8] Kerr, J, *Matters for Judgment,* pp.341–2; Barwick, G, Oral History Interview, NLA TRC 3317.

[9] Kerr, J, 'Conversation with Sir Anthony Mason During October–November 1975', Private Papers of Sir John Kerr, NAA M4523, 1 Part 14.

[10] 'Editorial: The Governor-general, the Judge and the Dismissal', *The Australian,* 28 August 2012.

[11] Barwick, G, to Kerr, J, 11 November 1982, NAA M4526, 4 Part 1; Kerr, J, to Barwick, G, 22 November 1982, NAA M4526, 4 Part 1.

[12] Kerr, JR, *Matters for Judgment,* p.341.

[13] Henderson, G, 'Kerr's Matter of Sound Judgment', *Sydney Morning Herald,* 8 January 1994, p.17; Henderson, G, *Menzies'*

Child: The Liberal Party of Australia, 1944–1994, Allen & Unwin, Sydney, 1994, p.224.

[14] Barwick, G, *Sir John Did His Duty;* Barwick, G, *A Radical Tory,* p.298.

[15] Kelly, P, *November 1975: The Inside Story of Australia's Greatest Political Crisis,* Allen & Unwin, Sydney, 1995, p.227.

[16] I interviewed Sir Anthony Mason twice during research for the second volume of my biography of Gough Whitlam, *Gough Whitlam: His Time,* however, he refused to discuss anything relating to the dismissal.

[17] Kerr, J, to Barwick, G, 9 November 1983, NAA M4526, 4 Part 1; Barwick, G, Oral History Interview, NLA TRC 3317.

3. WHAT DID MALCOLM FRASER KNOW?

[1] 'Sir John denies Fraser knew of intention', *Canberra Times,* 12 November 1975, pp.10, 14.

[2]   Reg Withers in Woolford, D, 'Key Figure in 1975 Dismissal Crisis, Reg Withers, Had Politics in His Blood', *The Australian,* 18 November 2014, www.theaustralia n.com.au/national-affairs/key-figur e-in-1975-dismissal-crisis-reg-with ers-had-politics-in-his-blood/story-fn59niix-1227127200480 (accessed 26 July 2015).

[3]   Ayres, P, *Malcolm Fraser,* p.293.

[4]   Fraser, M, and M Simons, *Malcolm Fraser: The Political Memoirs,* Melbourne University Press, Carlton, 2010, pp.422–3.

[5]   Confidential 'Loan Raisings: Possibility of a Public Inquiry', 4 July 1975, Loans Affair—Investigations: Possible Royal Commission, NAA M4081, 1/14.

[6]   Fraser, M, and M Simons, *Malcolm Fraser,* p.304.

[7]   Withers, R, Senate Hansard, 8 March 1973, p.291.

[8]   McMahon, W, in 'Whitlam Dismissal: Act Brought Greatest Disrepute', *The Canberra Times,* 5 February 1979, p.7.

[9] Robert Ashley, personal communication to the author, London, June 2015.

[10] McMahon, W, in 'Whitlam Dismissal: Act Brought Greatest Disrepute', p.7.

[11] Shand, A, Opinion: Executive Council—Overseas Borrowings, NAA M4524, 24. 'Opinions sent to the Governor-General on matters relating to the banks' response to the constitutional crisis of 1975', p.3.

[12] In contrast to Shand's conclusions regarding possible charges, the government's own advice from the Attorney-General's department's confidential briefing on the possible establishment of a Royal Commission into the loan raisings was that 'no charges of wrong doing would be sustained'. The department's opinion proved to be correct. The private prosecution against the four ministers, including Gough Whitlam, laid by the Sydney solicitor Danny Sankey and led

by David Rofe, failed on all counts.

[13] Hocking, J, *Gough Whitlam: His Time,* p.298; Fraser, M, and M Simons, *Malcolm Fraser,* p.304.

[14] Fraser, JM, in Hocking, J, *Gough Whitlam: His Time,* p.299.

[15] Fraser JM, Oral History Conversations Between JM Fraser and Clyde Cameron 1987. NLA TRC 2162, p.384. The interview was opened for public access in mid-2015.

[16] Kerr, JR, *Matters for Judgment,* p.240.

[17] Oakes, L, *Crash Through or Crash,* p.204.

[18] Kerr, JR, *Matters for Judgment,* p.348.

[19] See Kelly, P, *November 1975,* p.243; Fraser, M, and M Simons, *Malcolm Fraser,* p.297.

[20] Whitlam, EG, *The Truth of the Matter,* 2005 edition, p.139.

[21] Oakes, L, *Crash Through or Crash,* p.217; Kelly, P, *November 1975,* p.244.

[22] Reg Withers died on 15 November 2014.

4. AMBUSH: THE HALF-SENATE ELECTION

[1] Kerr, J, Notes on Conspiracy and Deceit Theory, M4524 2005, Item 6.

[2] Kerr, J, to G Barwick, 1 November 1983, NAA M4526, 4 Part 1.

[3] 'PM Counting on Rift in Opposition', *Sun Herald,* 19 October 1975, p.3.

[4] Confidential, Emerton, ID, 'Possible Half Senate Election', Cabinet and Parliamentary Division to the Prime Minister, 6 October 1975 (copy in possession of the author).

[5] Whitlam, EG, House of Representatives Hansard, 5 November 1975, p.2833.

[6] Ayres, P, *Malcolm Fraser,* p.293.

[7] Kelly, P, *The Unmaking of Gough,* p.294.

[8] Senator Pat Field had replaced ALP Senator Bert Milliner in Queensland, and Senator Cleaver Bunton had replaced ALP Senator Lionel Murphy in New South Wales. Although Cleaver Bunton

announced that he would not vote against Supply for the Whitlam government, neither appointment was the Labor party's nominated replacement, losing the ALP two crucial Senators in the divided Senate of 1975.

[9]   Ayres, P, *Malcolm Fraser,* p.299.

[10]   Whitlam, EG, 'Future Directions for Reform in Australia: Achieving Government through the House of Representatives Majority', John Curtin Memorial Lecture 1985, University of Western Australia, http://john.curtin.edu.au/jcmeml ect/whitlam1985.html (accessed 26 July 2015).

[11]   Ayres, P, *Malcolm Fraser,* p.299.

[12]   Fraser, A, 'The Extraordinary Day', *Quadrant,* December 1975, pp.4–18; 4.

[13]   Hocking, J, *Gough Whitlam: His Time,* p.338.

[14]   Ayres, P, *Malcolm Fraser,* p.291; Oakes, L, *Crash Through or Crash,* pp.182, 199. Oakes describes the half-Senate election as a major tactical pressure point on the Opposition in the

government's efforts to bring forward a vote on Supply.

[15] Kelly, P, *November 1975,* p.243.

[16] Barwick, G, *Sir John Did His Duty,* p.4.

[17] See Clark, A, 'The National Library Tapes', *The Sunday Age,* 15 October 2000, p.4. On the popular Whitlam dismissal website, the first reference in the chronology of events to Whitlam's decision to call the half-Senate election comes at 9am on 11 November 1975, http://whitlamdismissal.com/what-happened/brief-chronology (accessed 5 August 2015).

[18] Kerr, JR, 'Statement of Reasons'.

[19] Kerr, J, 'Statement by the Governor-General', Miscellaneous drafts following 11 November 1975, including a statement by HE [His Excellency] and draft of a letter to Mr Whitlam [Gough Whitlam], M4524 1 Part 10.

[20] Murphy, LK, Senate Hansard, April 1974, p.931.

[21]   The ALP national vote at the 1974 election fell just 0.29% for the House of Representatives.

[22]   Oral History Conversations Between JM Fraser and Clyde Cameron, 1987, NLA TRC 2162, p.379.

[23]   'The Whitlam Dismissal: Sir John was Wrong', Editorial, *Sydney Morning Herald,* 12 November 1975, www.smh.com.au/comment/the-age-editorial/the-whitlam-dismissal-sir-john-was-wrong-20141021-119du2.html (accessed 28 July 2015).

5. SIR JOHN KERR'S SECOND DISMISSAL

[1]   Kelly, P, and T Bramston, 'Kerr's Second Crisis', *The Australian,* 13 October 2012.

[2]   Menadue, J, 'Notice of Motion Written by Gough Whitlam 11 November 1975', NAA A1209 1975/2448.

[3]   Fraser, JM, House of Representatives Hansard, 11 November 1975, p.2928.

[4] Whitlam, EG, House of Representatives Hansard, 11 November 1975, p.2930.

[5] Robert Ashley, personal communication to the author, London, June 2015.

[6] Whitlam, EG, 'Why Labor Must Win', 16 November 1975, Whitlam Institute e-collection, http://cem.uws.edu.au/R/KGPVMGIVQE533RQMKLMC8IM2FCBYMFEAFXUE23TQMV21HMHTSY-00182?func=results-jump-full&set_entry=000003&set_number=000008&base=GEN01-EGW01 (accessed 23 August 2015).

[7] Fraser, M and M Simons, *Malcolm Fraser,* pp.307–8.

[8] Mungo MacCallum, political journalist and commentator, covered these events closely. MacCallum, M, 'The Dismissal: An Uncorrected Throwback to Tyranny', *The Drum,* 3 September 2012, abc.net.au/news/2012-09-03/maccallum-gough-dismissal/4239864 (accessed 23 August 2015).

6. 'A VERY BRITISH COUP'

Chapter title: The 1982 novel *A Very British Coup* (Hodder and Stoughton, London) by British Labour MP, Chris Mullin, tells the story of the brief tenure of a fictional British Labour Prime Minister.

[1]   British Foreign and Commonwealth Office (FCO), Memo, 'Australian Domestic Politics', Confidential, 17 October 1975, FCO 24/2051.

[2]   Evatt, HV, *The King and His Dominion Governors,* Frank Cass & Co, Sydney, (second edition), 1967, describes the prerogative power as 'usually regarded as having fallen into desuetude', p.247; Paul, J, 'The Head of State in Australia' says of the prerogative powers, 'while still extant in Britain, have seemed to fall into desuetude', https://www.samuelgriffith.org.au/papers/html/volume%201/chap9.htm (accessed 4 September 2017).

[3]   Sir Martin Charteris, the Queen's private secretary, to the Hon.

Gordon Scholes, Speaker of the House of Representatives, 17 November 1975, http://whitlamdi smissal.com/1975/11/17/letter-fro m-queens-private-secretary.html (accessed 4 September 2017). See also the statement by the British Foreign and Commonwealth Secretary to the Cabinet on 11 November 1975, 'The situation which had arisen in no way involved the UK Government. The Governor-General was responsible to the Queen in her capacity as The Queen of Australia', discussed at p.9 above.

[4] FCO to Certain Missions, 'Australian Constitutional Crisis', Restricted, 21 November 1975, FCO 24/2079. See the reassurance to the concerned President of Sierra Leone, drawing on the statement in the House of Commons of British Prime Minister Harold Wilson. High Commissioner to President Sierra Leone, 2 December 1975, FCO 24/2052.

[5]   British High Commission (BHC) to FCO, 'Priority Telegram No.873', 15 October 1975, FCO 24/2051.

[6]   Commonwealth of Australia Constitution Act, s.13, Rotation of Senators: 'The election to fill vacant places shall be made within one year before the places are to become vacant'. Half the Senate seats were to become vacant on 1 July 1976 and the election for that half-Senate could be called at any time from 1 July 1975. There were also four new Senate seats to be filled following the Whitlam government's successful passage of the *Senate (Representation of Territories) Act 1975*—two each for the Northern Territory and the ACT, together with two 'replacement Senators' who would also take up their places immediately as replacements for the ALP Senators Lionel Murphy and Bert Milliner. The pending half-Senate election would therefore be one of unusual mathematical complexity, even for that electorally Byzantine chamber,

and the six Senators to take up their seats immediately would give the ALP its best chance of securing a majority in the Senate, at least until the remaining Senators took their places in July 1976.

[7] FCO to BHC, 'Australian Constitutional Deadlock: Possible UK Involvement', Confidential, 28 October 1975, FCO 24/2079; FCO to BHC, 'The Australian Constitutional Deadlock', Confidential, 28 October 1975, FCO 24/2079. *See also* BHC to FCO, 'Australian Constitutional Deadlock: Possible Involvement of HMG', Confidential, 17 October 1975, FCO 24/2051; FCO, 'Australian Domestic Politics: Possible Intervention of the UK government', FCO 24/2051, 21 October 1975.

[8] Morrice James to FCO, 'Footnotes to the Constitutional Crisis', Confidential, 20 December 1975, FCO 24/2051.

[9] FCO, Memo to Legal Advisors, 'Australian Political Situation',

Confidential, 17 October 1975, FCO 24/2051; FCO to BHC, 'The Australian Constitutional Deadlock', Confidential, 28 October 1975, FCO 24/2051.

[10] The Colonial Office became the Commonwealth Office in 1966 and combined with the Foreign Office two years later to form the Foreign and Commonwealth Office.

[11] Stephens, T, 'We did but see her', *Sydney Morning Herald,* 7 February 2004, http://www.smh.com.au/articles/2004/02/06/1075854066586.html (accessed 10 August 2017). Menzies was quoting the seventeenth-century poet Thomas Ford.

[12] 'Meeting between the Prime Minister and the Australian leader of the Opposition'. 19 June 1973, Personal and Confidential, Prime Minister's Office Files in The UK National Archives (PREM) 15/1304.

[13] Prime Minister's Office (PMO) to FCO, Personal and Confidential, 21 June 1972, PREM 15/1304.

[14]   FCO   to   PMO,   'Australian Constitutional   Issues', Confidential, 21 June 1972, PREM 15/1304.

[15]   ibid.

[16]   Edmund Campion, 'Armstrong, John   Ignatius   (1908–1977)', *Australian   Dictionary   of Biography,* National Centre of Biography, Australian National University, http://adb.anu.edu.au /biography/armstrong-john-ignati us-9384/text16487   (published first in hardcopy 1993, accessed online 24 August 2017).

[17]   FCO   to   PMO,   'Australian Constitutional   Issues', Confidential, 21 June 1972, PREM 15/1304.

[18]   'On arrival he [Murphy] made one   or   two   provocative statements to the press about "relics of colonialism"', Document 441, Letter Greenhill to James, Personal   and   Confidential, *Documents in Australian Foreign Policy,* Vol.27, *Australia and the United Kingdom 1960–1975.*

[19]   ibid, Note for the Record by James, Confidential, 23 May 1974, Document 480.

[20]   Downer, A, to Heath, E, Personal letter, 11 June 1973, PREM 15/1304.

[21]   Hancock, I R, 'Downer, Sir Alexander Russell (Alick) (1910–1981)', *Australian Dictionary of Biography,* National Centre of Biography, Australian National University, http://adb.anu.edu.au/biography/downer-sir-alexander-russell-alick-12434/text22357 (published first in hardcopy 2007, accessed online 28 August 2017).

[22]   Hocking, J, *Gough Whitlam: His Time,* The Miegunyah Press, Carlton, 2014, p.41.

[23]   PMO to FCO, 'Meeting with Sir Alexander Downer', 22 June 1973, PREM 15/1304.

[24]   'Meeting with Premiers of Queensland and Western Australia', 31 January 1975, FCO 24/2076.

[25]   Kerr, R, to Callaghan, J, Letter, 9 April 1975, FCO 24/2078.

[26]   Twomey, A, 'The States, the
Commonwealth and the
Crown—the Battle for
Sovereignty', Papers on
Parliament, No.48, January 2008,
http://www.aph.gov.au/About_Pa
rliament/Senate/Research_and_E
ducation/pops/pop48/~/link.aspx
?_id=76D508CC96314F19A37117
1C7A270930&_z=z (accessed 24
August 2017).

[27]   The Whitlam government's *Royal
Style and Titles Act 1973*
amended the Royal title, with the
Queen's concurrence and
support, to 'Elizabeth II, Queen
of Australia and Her other
Realms and Territories, Head of
the Commonwealth'. See the
discussion by the Museum of
Australian Democracy of the key
differences in the Whitlam
government's change to the
Royal title as previously styled
under the Menzies government's
Royal Style and Titles Act 1953
at http://www.foundingdocs.gov.
au/item-did-28.html (accessed 25
July 2017).

[28] FCO to Certain Missions, Restricted, 'The Australian Constitutional Crisis', 21 November 1975, FCO 24/2079. Whitlam described the state governments as 'governments of British colonies'.

[29] BHC (British High Commission) to FCO, 'Telling the Feds and States', Confidential, 31 January 1975, FCO 24/2076.

[30] Record by Wright of Meeting of Prime Ministers, 'Australian Constitutional Issues', Confidential, 20 December 1974, Document 497; Note for the Record by James, Confidential, 23 May 1974, Document 480, both in *Documents in Australian Foreign Policy,* op. cit., Vol.27; FCO, 'Australian Constitutional issues', Confidential, 22 September 1975, FCO 24/2032.

[31] Briefing Notes by Emerton for Prime Minister's Discussions in London, 11 December 1974, Document 493, and FCO Brief AMV(74) J4, 12 December 1974. Document 494, both in

Documents in Australian Foreign Policy, op. cit., Vol.27.

[32]   Gough Whitlam, PM, Press Conference, Vigyan Bhavan, New Delhi, 6 June 1973, PM Transcripts, http://pmtranscripts .pmc.gov.au/taxonomy/term/14? page=102 (accessed 28 July 2017).

[33]   Record by Wright of Meeting of Prime Ministers, 20 December 1974, Document 497 in *Documents in Australian Foreign Policy,* op. cit., Vol.27.

[34]   Letter Holt to Wilson. 24 August 1967. Document 423 in *Documents in Australian Foreign Policy,* op.cit., Vol.27.

[35]   Telegram, Commonwealth office to Canberra, 27 August 1967, Document 424 in *Documents in Australian Foreign Policy,* op.cit., Vol.27.

[36]   FCO, 'Australian Constitutional Issues', Confidential, 22 September 1975, FCO 24/2032.

[37]   Charteris to Bunting, 24 April 1973, Document 459 in

Documents in Australian Foreign Policy, op. cit., Vol.27.

[38] FCO, 'Record of Meeting between Prime Ministers', Confidential, 20 December 1974, FCO 24/2059. The spectre of the Queen receiving conflicting advice on state matters was only resolved in 1986 with the passage of the Australia Act, Twomey, A, 'Constitutional convention and constitutional reality', Vol.78, *Australian Law Journal,* 798 2004, p.803.

[39] FCO, 'Record of Meeting between Prime Ministers', Confidential, 20 December 1974, FCO 24/2059.

[40] Murphy, P, *Monarchy and the End of Empire: The House of Windsor, the British Government, and the Postwar Commonwealth,* Oxford University Press, Oxford, 2013. Chapter 9; FCO, 'Australian Constitutional Issues', Confidential, 22 September 1975, FCO 24/2032.

[41] Murphy, ibid.

[42] ibid., Chapter 9. Royal involvement in policy can also

be seen in recent revelations, which the Palace had sought to block, that Prince Charles lobbied British Prime Minister Tony Blair on government policies in the 2000s.

[43] Minute, Wilford to Brimelow, 'UK/Australian constitutional problems', Confidential, 22 October 1974, Document 487; Charteris to Bridges, Personal and Confidential, 6 December 1974, Document 491 both in *Documents in Australian Foreign Policy,* op. cit., Vol.27; BHC to FCO, 'Australian Constitutional Issues', Confidential, FCO 24/2059.

[44] See for instance Letter, Charteris to Acland, 25 October 1974, Document 488 in *Documents in Australian Foreign Policy,* op.cit., Vol.27; 'advice with a small "a"' in Letter, Charteris to Bridges, Personal and Confidential, 6 December 1974, Document 491 in *Documents in Australian Foreign Policy,* op. cit., Vol.27. Charteris asked to be kept

informed 'about any situation that might possibly lead to the tendering of conflicting advice to the Queen', in BHC to FCO, 'The Australian Constitutional Deadlock: Possible Involvement of HMG', Confidential, 17 October 1975, FCO 24/2074.

[45]   FCO Memo, Confidential, 6 January 1975, FCO 24/2059.

[46]   Charteris to Bunting, 24 April 1973, Document 459 in *Documents in Australian Foreign Policy,* op. cit., Vol.2.

[47]   Murphy, op. cit. See in particular the discussion in Chapter 9, p.146.

[48]   FCO 24/2078, Inside cover, 'useful information related to contents of this file', FCO 24/2078.

[49]   'Supply bills. Liberal decision possible today', *Canberra Times,* 14 October 1975, p.3; Hocking, *Gough Whitlam: It's Time,* p.261.

[50]   Hocking, ibid, p.260.

[51]   '"Device" Fraser says', *Canberra Times,* 17 October 1975, p.11.

[52] *Commonwealth of Australia Constitution Act* s.11. The Senate may proceed to the despatch of business, notwithstanding the failure of any State to provide for its representation in the Senate.

[53] O'Leary, T, 'The Supply Crisis. Tight lips on tactics. Poll decision rests with PM', *Canberra Times,* 16 October 1975, p.11.

[54] ibid.

[55] BHC to FCO, 'Australian Political Situation', Confidential, 7 November 1975, FCO 24/2051.

[56] BHC to FCO, Confidential, 10 October 1975, 'I made the excuse of a Constitutional query to discuss the position with Senator Chaney', FCO 24/2051.

[57] Ayres, P, *Malcolm Fraser: A Biography,* William Heinemann Australia, Melbourne, 1987, p.299.

[58] BHC to FCO, 'Australian Political Situation', Confidential, 7 November 1975, FCO 24/2051.

[59] BHC to FCO, Confidential, 24 October 1975, FCO 24/2051.

[60]	FCO Memo, Confidential, 'Australian Political Situation', 28 October 1975, FCO 24/2051.

[61]	BHC to FCO, 7 November 1975, FCO 24/2074; BHC to FCO, Confidential, 31 October 1975, FCO 24/2051.

[62]	ibid., 7 November 1975.

[63]	16th October Confidential by telegram Australian political situation; BHC to FCO, 17 October 1975, FCO 24/2051.

[64]	Twomey, 'The States, the Commonwealth and the Crown—the Battle for Sovereignty', op cit.

[65]	BHC to FCO Priority telegram No.876, 16 October 1975, FCO 24/2015; FCO to BHC, Australian Constitutional Deadlock, Confidential, 28 October 1975, FCO 24/2015.

[66]	Under-Secretary of State for External Affairs, Ottawa to Canadian High Commission, Canberra, 'Conversation with Senator Eugene Forsey', 28 November 1975, FCO 24/2052.

[67] Kerr, J R, Preface, *Matters for Judgment: An Autobiography*, Macmillan, South Melbourne, 1978, 'Epilogue' by Senator Eugene Forsey.

[68] BHC to FCO, 'The Australian Constitutional Deadlock: Possible Involvement of HMG', Confidential, 17 October 1975, FCO.

[69] Emerton, I, 'Possible Half-Senate Election', Confidential, 6 October 1975, in Attorney-General's Department, 'The Dismissal—Advice—Compelling the States to act regarding issuing of writs for a half Senate election', NAA M4081 2/2.

[70] BHC to FCO, 'Note for Record', Confidential, 17 October 1975, FCO 24/2051.

[71] ibid.

[72] ibid.

[73] See King George to Prime Minister Scullin in 1930 regarding Scullin's appointment of Sir Isaac Isaacs as Governor-General which the King vehemently opposed, 'being a constitutional

monarch I must, Mr Scullin, accept your advice'. Crisp, L F, 'The appointment of Sir Isaac Isaacs as Governor-General of Australia 1930', *Historical Studies,* Melbourne, 1964, 253–7, p.257.

[74] Confidential, 'Australian Domestic Politics: Possible Intervention of the UK Government', 21 October 1975, FCO 24/2051.

[75] See the discussion at Chapter 1 above.

[76] Kelly, P, and T Bramston, *The Dismissal,* Penguin Books, Melbourne, 2015, p.125.

[77] Smith, D, 'Address by Sir David Smith', 7 November 2004, Old Parliament House, https://dismis sed.moadoph.gov.au/docs/sir-da vid-smith-address.pdf p.9 (my emphasis) (accessed 24 August 2017). The British High Commissioner similarly noted that, 'a factor which had been very much in Sir J. Kerr's mind had been the need to protect The Queen' and 'his obvious wish to avoid drawing The Queen

directly into Australian politics', [BHC to FCO (Morrice James), 'Footnotes to the Constitutional Crisis', Confidential, 20 December 1975, FCO 24/2052].

[78]   FCO, 'Australian Domestic Politics', Confidential, 17 October 1975, FCO 24/2074.

[79]   FCO to BHC (Morrice James), 'Australian Constitutional Deadlock: Possible UK Involvement', Confidential, 28 October 1975, FCO 24/2079.

[80]   The vice-regal notices published the following day confirm that the meeting took place at Government House, Vice-Regal, Canberra Times, 17 October 1975, p.2; Draft Palliser itinerary, FCO 24/2032.

[81]   Sir Roden Cutler, Oral History Interview, NLA ORAL TRC 2834. Kerr was Lieutenant Governor of NSW.

[82]   BHC to FCO, 'Australian Constitutional Deadlock: Possible Involvement of HMG', Confidential, 20 October 1975, attachment to FCO Confidential,

'Australian Constitutional Deadlock: Possible UK Involvement', 24 October 1975, FCO 24/2079.

[83] Sir Roden Cutler, Oral History Interview, NLA ORAL TRC 2834.

[84] FCO, Memo, 'Australia: Constitutional Crisis', Confidential, 24 October 1975, FCO 24/2051.

[85] Kerr, *Matters for Judgment,* p.330; BHC to FCO, 'Footnotes to the Constitutional Crisis', Confidential, 20 December 1975, FCO 24/2051.

[86] BHC to FCO, 'Footnotes to the Constitutional Crisis', Confidential, 20 December 1975, FCO 24/2052.

[87] BHC (Morrice James) to FCO, 'Footnotes to the Constitutional Crisis', Confidential, 20 December 1975, FCO 24/2052.

[88] Murphy, P, op. cit., Chapter 9.

[89] High Commissioner to President Sierra Leone, 2 December 1975, FCO 24/2052.

7. 'THE MAN WHO WOULD BE KING'

[1]   Blackstone, W, *Blackstone's Commentaries on the Laws of England,* The Lawbook Exchange, Clark, New Jersey, p.1231.

[2]   Denny, Captain WT, 'A Summary of Events Surrounding the Dismissal of the Prime Minister E.G. Whitlam on 11 November 1975', copy in possession of the author.

[3]   Bill Denny, interview with the author, 2 March 2010.

[4]   ibid.

[5]   Denny, Captain WT, 'A Summary of Events Surrounding the Dismissal of the Prime Minister E.G. Whitlam on 11 November 1975'.

[6]   Bill Denny, interview with the author, 2 March 2010.

[7]   SBS, 'The Paradoxical Malcolm Fraser', http://www.sbs.com.au/news/article/2015/03/20/paradoxical-malcolm-fraser (accessed 20 March 2015).

[8]   Ziegler, Philip, *Mountbatten: The Official Biography,* Phoenix Press, California, 2001, p.657.

[9]   Smith, D to Kerr, J, Archives [Arrangements relating to the disposition of Sir John Kerr's records with the National Archives of Australia], 15 January 1981, NAA M4520 2.

[10] *Sydney Morning Herald,* 24 December 1975, p.1; Charteris, M, to Bunting, J, *Letter from Sir Martin Charteris,* 9 January 1976, NAA M4524 1 Part 6.

[11] Kelly, P and T Bramston, *The Dismissal,* Viking, 2015.

[12] See Sir William Heseltine's comment that the Queen would have advised Kerr 'not to act *when he did'.* [My emphasis] Stephens, T, 'Buckingham Palace Regrets', *The Age,* 10 March 2001; Quekett, M, 'No Wake-up Call for Queen over Dismissal', *The West Australian,* 12 April 2011, http://whitlamdismissal.com/2011/04/12/how-the-queen-heard-about-whitlam-dismissal.htm

l#more-664 (accessed 28 March 2016).

[13] Kelly, P and T Bramston, 'The Queen Wanted Kerr Gone Soon after Whitlam's Dismissal', *The Australian,* 7 November 2015, p.1.

[14] Kerr, J, 'The Queen's visit and the position of the Governor-General', Personal and Confidential Papers of Sir John Kerr: Assessment of position of the Queen's visit and relevant conversations, NAA M4524, 34.

[15] Kerr, J to Fraser, JM, 10 June 1977, Correspondence between the Prime Minister and the Governor-General on the Governor-General's resignation, NAA 4524 31.

[16] Menzies, RG, St Andrew's Dinner, 27 November 1976, Melbourne. Recording at NLA MS4936.

[17] Hocking, J, *Gough Whitlam: His Time,* p.390.

[18] Billy Snedden, Oral History Interview, NLA ORAL TRC 4900/57 1983/7.

[19] 'A Cow of a Day for Kerr', *The Age,* 21 March 1977, p.1.

[20] 'Age Writer Wins Award', *The Canberra Times,* 3 November 1977, p.7.

[21] Rod Johnson, VRC Chief Executive, 1986–94, in 'Sir John Kerr in Fine Form at the 1977 Melbourne Cup', YouTube (accessed 3 April 2016).

[22] Whitlam, EG, *The Truth of the Matter,* p.240.

[23] Kerr, J to Fraser, JM, Correspondence between the Prime Minister and the Governor-General on the Governor-General's resignation, 10 June 1977, NAA 4524 31; Kerr, J, *Matters for Judgment,* p.421.

[24] Miller, Harry M, *Confessions of a Not So Secret Agent,* Hachette, Sydney, 2009, p.192.

[25] Kerr, J, *Matters for Judgment,* p.ix.

[26] Greenwood Challoner & Co to Harry M Miller, Correspondence with Allen Allen & Hemsley,

Solicitors and Notaries, 16 September 1977, NAA M4507 40.

[27] Greenwood Challoner & Co to Harry M Miller, Correspondence with Allen Allen & Hemsley, Solicitors and Notaries, 16 September 1977, NAA M4507 40.

[28] Greenwood Challoner & Co to Harry M Miller, Correspondence with Allen Allen & Hemsley, Solicitors and Notaries, 16 September 1977, NAA M4507 40.

[29] Allen Allen & Hemsley to Kerr, Sir John, Correspondence with Allen Allen & Hemsley, Solicitors and Notaries, 17 November 1977, NAA M4507 40.

[30] *Allen Allen & Hemsley v. Deputy Federal Commissioner of Taxation & Ors,* Federal Court of Australia, 2 September 1988.

[31] ibid.

[32] JF Chown & Company Limited, 'Note on Section 487 Taxes Act 1970: Mr Federick King', Correspondence with Allen Allen & Hemsley, Solicitors and Notaries, NAA M4507 40.

[33]   Aprolon was incorporated on 30 November 1977, https://www.du edil.com/company/01341472/apr olon-limited (accessed 26 March 2016).

[34]   Allen Allen & Hemsley, 'Telex Attention: Tony Carter', Correspondence with Allen Allen & Hemsley, Solicitors and Notaries, 8 December 1977, NAA M4507 40.

[35]   Edmonds, RF, Allen Allen & Hemsley to Kerr, JR, Correspondence with Allen Allen & Hemsley, Solicitors and Notaries, 17 November 1977, NAA M4507 40.

[36]   Edmonds, RF, Allen Allen & Hemsley to Kerr, JR, Correspondence with Allen Allen & Hemsley, Solicitors and Notaries, 17 November 1977, NAA M4507 40.

[37]   Yeend, G to Prime Minister, Resignation correspondence, 18 April 1977, NAA M4524 1 Part 5; Ramsey, A, 'A head of state who couldn't handle mud',

Sydney Morning Herald, 14 May 2003, p.15.

[38]   Greenwood Challoner & Co to Harry M Miller, Correspondence with Allen Allen & Hemsley, Solicitors and Notaries, 16 September 1977, NAA M4507 40.

[39]   Edmonds, RF, Allen Allen & Hemsley to Kerr, JR, Correspondence with Allen Allen & Hemsley, Solicitors and Notaries, 17 November 1977, NAA M4507 40.

[40]   Prime Minister 'Australian Ambassador to UNESCO' *Press Release,* 9 February 1978. UNESCO: United Nations Educational, Scientific and Cultural Organisation.

[41]   Cameron, C, House of Representatives Hansard, 22 February 1978, pp.95–6.

[42]   Hocking, J, *Gough Whitlam: His Time,* p.397.

[43]   Keating, PJ, House of Representatives Hansard, 22 February 1978, p.31; McClelland, J, Senate Hansard, 22 February 1978, p.47.

[44] Fraser, JM, 'Statement to the House', House of Representatives Hansard, 2 March 1978, http://whitlamdismissal.com/1978/03/02/kerr-quits-unesco-post.html (accessed 30 March 2016).

[45] Hocking, J, *Gough Whitlam: His Time,* pp.423–52.

[46] Ayres, P, *Malcolm Fraser,* p.323; Simons, M and M Fraser, *Malcolm Fraser,* p.335.

[47] Fraser, JM, House of Representatives Hansard, 22 February 1978, p.31.

[48] Kerr, J, *Matters for Judgment,* pp.418–20.

[49] ibid., p.430.

[50] Yeend, G to Kerr, J, 8 July 1977, NAA M4524 1 Part 5.

[51] Fraser, M, Resignation of the Governor-General and appointment of his successor, 14 July 1977, http://pmtranscripts.dpmc.gov.au/release/transcript-4441 (accessed 3 April 2016).

[52] Earlier versions of this have been made in Hocking, J, 'The Governor-General, the Palace and the Dismissal of Gough Whitlam:

The Mysterious Case of "the Palace Letters"', *Crikey,* 22 February 2016; Hocking, J, 'We Won't Know The Full History Of The Dismissal Until The Queen Says So', *The Huffington Post,* 11 November 2015, http://www .huffingtonpost.com.au/jenny-hoc king/the-dismissal_b_8516530.ht ml.

[53] Smith, D to Kerr, J, Archives [Arrangements relating to the disposition of Sir John Kerr's records with the National Archives of Australia], 20 May 1980, NAA M4520 2.

BACK COVER MATERIAL

'Shocking, compelling, and profoundly important'
ANNA FUNDER

Here is the definitive story of the most divisive episode in Australia's history—the dismissal of Gough Whitlam's Labor government.

In her award-winning biography of Gough Whitlam, Jenny Hocking exposed the astonishing unknown story of the planning and the people behind the dismissal. Never before released material from Sir John Kerr's private papers revealed the secret role of High Court justice Sir Anthony Mason and Kerr's collusion with Malcolm Fraser.

Now, Hocking's forensic investigations reveal explosive files in the UK National Archives that add a disturbing dimension to this untold story.

Hocking reveals the Palace connection and unravels the web of intrigue behind the British Foreign and Commonwealth Office's link to the dismissal of the Whitlam government in the name of the Queen. She brilliantly brings together this hidden history—a mixture of the unknown, the overlooked and the clandestine—to write a political thriller: the story you were never meant to know.

www.ingramcontent.com/pod-product-compliance
Lightning Source LLC
Chambersburg PA
CBHW070803270326
41927CB00010B/2262